'Kehinde Andrews's compelling research highlights the trajectories of identity-building, resistance to racism, and engagement with the state for many from Britain's Black communities. Those interested in racial equality, education, organizing and commun[...] and insight in thi[...]

Dr Rob Berkeley, Dire[...]

'This is a major contribution to the field that extends our appreciation of the challenges that education faces from racism in the twenty-first century. It deserves to be read not only by educationalists but by all those who have an interest in the principles of diversity, equality and inclusivity and the creation of a just and fair society for all, irrespective of their ethnicity, faith or gender.'

Dame Jocelyn Barrow, DBE

'The elegance of this work by Kehinde Andrews is demonstrated by the skilful way in which he has opened our understanding to the dynamic nature and the development of the Black supplementary school movement. The book highlights the role that Black supplementary schools play in combating inequalities in education and in ensuring success for Black children in mainstream schooling. This is an essential read for all committed to the goal of education for all.'

Dr Keith Davidson, Management and Leadership Practitioner and education author

Resisting Racism

For Nicole, Assata, and Kadiri

Resisting Racism

Race, inequality, and the Black supplementary school movement

Kehinde Andrews

A Trentham Book
Institute of Education Press

First published in 2013 by the Institute of Education Press, University of London, 20 Bedford Way, London WC1H 0AL
www.ioe.ac.uk/ioepress

© Kehinde Andrews 2013

British Library Cataloguing-in-Publication Data
A catalogue record for this book is available from the British Library

ISBNs
978-1-85856-515-6 (paperback)
978-1-85856-537-8 (PDF eBook)
978-1-85856-538-5 (ePub eBook)
978-1-85856-539-2 (Kindle eBook)

All rights reserved. No part of this publication may be reproduced, stored in a retrieval system, or transmitted in any form or by any means, electronic, mechanical, photocopying, recording, or otherwise, without the prior permission of the copyright owner.

Every effort has been made to trace copyright holders and to obtain their permission for the use of copyright material. The publisher apologizes for any errors or omissions and would be grateful if notified of any corrections that should be incorporated in future reprints or editions of this book.

The opinions expressed in this publication are those of the authors and do not necessarily reflect the views of the Institute of Education, University of London.

Typeset by Quadrant Infotech (India) Pvt Ltd
Printed by CPI Group (UK) Ltd, Croydon, CR0 4YY

Contents

Acknowledgements	viii
About the author	ix
Introduction: Why Black supplementary schools?	1

Part One: The Black supplementary school movement

Chapter 1: Researching the movement	10
Chapter 2: The role of Blackness	22
Chapter 3: The organization and philosophies of supplementary schools	39
Chapter 4: Mainstream educational discourse in the official projects	60
Chapter 5: The self-help challenge to the mainstream school system	75

Part Two: The Lumumba School Study

Chapter 6: Researching the Lumumba School	92
Chapter 7: The Lumumba Saturday School: An ethnographic study	99
Chapter 8: Lessons from the Lumumba	120
Conclusion: Resisting racism	132
Appendix	137
References	141
Index	151

Acknowledgements

I would like to thank everyone who has taken part in this research, which without your valuable insights would have been impossible to complete.

I would especially like to thank Menelik, Kamili, and Kemi and all of the children and parents at the Lumumba Saturday School for allowing me to be a part of the programme.

Special thanks to Professor Margaret Clark for all of her time and effort in helping me put together the manuscript. Also, I would like to thank my colleagues at Newman University for supporting me while I was writing the book, with particular thanks to Dr Gillian McGillivray.

This book could not have been completed without the assistance of the George Padmore Archive, London. I would particularly like to thank Sarah Garrod, who painstakingly tracked down all of the archive files I requested.

Many thanks to Nia Imara of the National Association of Black Supplementary Schools for the interview and list of contacts, and for the tireless effort of putting together the directory.

Many thanks to Dr Gillian Klein of Trentham Books for her painstaking copy-editing of the manuscript.

Of course, I also could not have completed this book without the support of my family, with a special thanks to my mom and dad, and to my lovely wife Nicole, who has been my rock throughout.

About the author

Kehinde Andrews is Senior Lecturer in Working with Children, Young People, and Families, and Criminology, at Newman University. He received his PhD from the University of Birmingham in Sociology and Cultural Studies. His research interests are in contemporary manifestations of Black radicalism and how minority communities organize to respond to discrimination and inequality.

Introduction
Why Black supplementary schools?

This book presents an account of the Black supplementary school movement in Britain. The grassroots and fragmented nature of the movement makes it impossible to estimate the exact number of Black supplementary schools or to give a clear picture of all of the different types of programmes. However, the book presents a comprehensive analysis of the emergence of Black supplementary schools, their different forms, and the underlying tensions and debates within the movement. It begins by locating the development of supplementary schools in the Black community.

Although there has been a Black presence in Britain since at least the occupation by the Roman Empire, mass migration of people from the Caribbean began with the *Windrush* in 1948. Yet it was not until almost 20 years later that the first Black supplementary school opened as the nature of Caribbean settlement in the UK changed.

With its labour force decimated by the Second World War, Britain needed to draw on her Empire for workers, so the borders were opened to people from across the Commonwealth (Mason, 1995). It was the first time the British public had come into contact with large numbers of Black and Asian subjects of the British crown.

This was not, however, the first contribution that people of the Empire had made to Britain. Slavery and colonialism had provided the materials and the 'labour' that fuelled the industrial revolution which modernized Britain (Gillen and Ghosh, 2007; Williams, 1975). The exploitation of resources and markets for British goods continued to provide wealth for Britain, whose prosperity was due largely to the 'empire where the sun never sets' (Tiejun, 2007: 12). What has made Britain cannot be separated from her colonial conquests. Even the quintessential icon of British culture, the cup of tea, is a product of leaves from India or Ceylon, sweetened with sugar produced in the Caribbean (Hall, 1991).

As subjects of the British crown, those in the Empire served in both World Wars, and contributed in many ways to the war efforts (Jackson, 2006). There was contact between Caribbean people and the British public before the war, when Caribbean servicemen were stationed in Britain and served in all sections of the armed forces (Phillips and Phillips, 1998). As one Caribbean ex-serviceman said about the involvement in the Second World War, Caribbean people 'did our bit' (*ibid*.: 26). British society and history are inextricably connected and indebted to the people of the Empire.

This dependence on the Empire helps to explain why Britain chose to invite large numbers of Black and Asian people to the country. Racist beliefs in the superiority of White people were not at the time the niche perspective of far-right groups, as they (presumably) are today. White superiority was an accepted and commonplace view, espoused, for example, by Winston Churchill (Roy, 2003: 58). Reaching out to the Empire was a continuation of a relationship based on Britain's use of the colonies and its people for her own benefit. The work Black and Asian people were brought in to do, regardless of their education and experience, was largely unskilled and at the lower end of the job market. Such work was 'often dirty, poorly paid and involved unsocial hours like night shift working' (Mason, 1995: 24).

The racial inequality in the labour market has had a lasting effect on the position of ethnic minorities in Britain (Berthoud, 2000). Opening her borders was certainly not a benevolent act. The settlement that followed was an unintended, and often seen as an unwelcome, consequence of migration.

When Britain passed the British Nationalities Act in 1948, the aim was not for people who had migrated to settle in the United Kingdom (Mason, 1995). Citizenship was granted to those from the former Empire, now the Commonwealth, to allow these subjects to work and fill the labour shortage, and it was expected that they would return to their home countries once this work was no longer required. This was also the rationale of the people from the Caribbean: they aimed to migrate, find work to earn money to send home, and eventually return to their islands (Phillips and Phillips, 1998). Consequently, the first to arrive were mostly men, who were either single or supporting families in their home countries. The nature and expectations of the early Caribbean migrants were based on these hopes of one day returning.

Settlement

The first wave of Caribbean migrants faced overt abuse and were kept at the bottom rung of the jobs ladder. Such discrimination is commonplace for migrants and is almost expected (International Labour Office, 1999). Not that this justifies either the racism faced by the early migrants or their efforts to resist it. However, when you have no settled roots in a society and no family to protect, it is not essential to create organized resistance. Between 1948 and 1955 the number of migrants from the Caribbean was not large:

in 1951 there were approximately 15,000 Caribbeans in Britain (Phillips and Phillips, 1998). Consequently, the development of a community as a source of resistance was also at an early stage. It was during the second wave of migration from the Caribbean that the community and its relationship to British society began to change, with migration to Britain peaking from 1955 to 1962.

What was important during this period was not just the numbers of migrants but also the fact that they came as families, bringing their children. The profile of Caribbean immigrants changed from migrant workers, intent on returning to their home countries, to a settler community putting down roots in Britain. The dynamics therefore shifted as they built communities in the urban conurbations of the country. The governments of the period responded to this change by restricting immigration from what they termed 'New Commonwealth' countries, where the Black and Asian subjects lived (Mason, 1995). With the government legislating against the growing presence of Black and Asian people in the country and the increasing hostility from the White population due to the larger communities, a distinct identity of difference began to arise in the Caribbean population. In the words of Phillips and Phillips (1998: 256):

> Caribbean migrants became black people during the decade of the sixties, and by the end of the seventies we had begun to share the same assumptions about our national status as our white compatriots. That is to say, we became black Britons. This was a fundamental change, driven by the generations who had arrived as children, or had been born in Britain.

As generations of Caribbeans settled and were born in Britain, they began to see themselves as British, as equals who deserved equality under the law. Importantly, Blackness became the route for this identification, due in part to the experience of racism and therefore the recognition of their outsider status.

Since Caribbean people decided to settle, generations of Caribbean children have been born both in and outside Britain who have experienced the school system. The parents of the first children to go to British schools had faith in the school system to educate their young (Yekwai, 1998). There was little reason to doubt the quality of the education offered, as their only experience of British schooling was the elite private schools in the Caribbean. Education was seen as a key tool for Caribbean children to use to advance in society and escape the unskilled work at the lower end of the labour market to which their parents had been consigned (Stone, 1981). So not only did they trust the school system but they believed it would benefit the lives of their children.

Contrary to stereotyped portrayals of African Caribbean families, there has always been a strong emphasis on achieving in education, starting with the first generation of migrants. This is no different from other immigrant groups who move to wealthier countries in order to secure work, a higher standard of living, and better educational opportunities for their children (Adams and Kirova, 2006). However, this faith in the school system to provide an education and a solid foundation for future success was misplaced, as 'the school experience began as a trauma for the majority of black schoolchildren and went on to be a rallying point and radicalizing issue for their parents' (Phillips and Phillips, 1998: 257).

Educationally subnormal

In 1971 Bernard Coard, a Grenadian teacher, wrote a book entitled *How the West Indian Child is Made Educationally Subnormal in the British School System*, which forever shattered the myth that the British system was a bastion of equality. The book received a great deal of publicity because it openly denounced the practices of British schooling with regard to Black children. Coard was featured in the national press, including *The Times Educational Supplement* and the *New Statesman*. The impact of the book on the Black community was fundamental, as it broke the faith in mainstream schooling and contributed to mass resistance to educational inequality.

That is not to say that before the book was published Black parents were ignorant as to what was happening in the schools, blindly allowing their children to be discriminated against. In fact, Coard was commissioned to write the book by the Caribbean Education and Community Workers Association (CECWA), comprising people working in Black communities and the parents of schoolchildren. The issue of how Black children were being treated in schools was also raised by the North London West Indian Association in 1965 (Tomlinson, 1988), and the Black supplementary school movement predates the publishing of the book.

Therefore, the resistance to racism in schooling, which was a significant feature of Black community life from the 1970s onwards, would have occurred without the publication of Coard's book. However, the attention the book brought to the issue sparked resistance across the country (Issa and Williams, 2009). The insightful analysis provided by Coard framed the discussion for years to come.

Coard's thesis was that African Caribbean children were disproportionately failing in mainstream schooling because of the school system itself. Coard drew attention to the overwhelmingly excessive placement of Black children in schools for the 'educationally subnormal' (ESN). Students within these schools were deemed incapable of academic success, so expectations of them were low and their opportunities severely curtailed. Black children were being misidentified as ESN due to the cultural bias of the IQ tests used and the low expectations of them held by teachers. In some parts of London up to 70 per cent of Black Caribbean students were labelled as ESN (Dove, 1993). This limitation of Black students to restricted forms of education has been a major criticism of the mainstream school system, leading to protests against busing and banding in Haringey in the 1970s.

Central to Coard's analysis was the role played by teachers in creating the failure of Black children. According to Coard (1971: 18):

> There are three main ways in which a teacher can seriously affect the performance of a Black child: by being openly prejudiced, by being patronizing, and by having low expectations of a child's abilities. All three attitudes can be found among teachers in this country. Indeed these attitudes are widespread.

Importantly, only the first of these (open discrimination) involves teachers acting on overt racial prejudice. Coard described patronizing teachers as 'the sort who treat a Black child like a favourite pet animal', appearing well meaning in their praise, as in 'he is very bright for a coloured boy' (*ibid.*: 19). Coard argued that such attitudes led to teachers viewing the children as educationally subnormal and restricting them to only remedial and low-level education. Contemporary scholars, too, argue that low teacher expectation creates a self-fulfilling prophecy in which Black children underperform because they are expected to do so (*Inter alia* Byfield, 2008; Howarth, 2004).

Coard was also highly critical of the emphasis placed on the use of the Queen's English in schools, and especially in forms of assessment, including the IQ test. African Caribbean children at the time were using colloquial Caribbean dialects such as Patois. Their language was rejected by the schools, which set the children up for failure. More recent Black commentators such as Carter (2003) and Figueroa (1991) have analysed the way that schools reject the cultural capital of Black children and how this works to marginalize the students.

According to Coard (1971: 30), the school curriculum also affected Black students because the lack of any Black history led to Black self-hatred and a psychological crisis in the students, which further disadvantaged them:

> When the pictures, illustrations, music, heroes, great historical, and contemporary figures in the classroom are all White, it is difficult for a child to identify with anyone who is not White. When in addition the pictures of Blacks are golliwog stereotypes, about whom filthy jokes are made; when most plays show Black men doing servant jobs; when the word 'Black' in every story is synonymous with evil, then it becomes impossible for the child to want to be Black ... the Black child under these influences develops a deep inferiority complex. He soon loses motivation to succeed academically since, at best, the learning experience in the classroom is an elaborate irrelevance to his personal life, and at worst it is a racially humiliating experience.

Inspiration for the Black self-hatred argument was drawn from the seminal Clark and Clark (1940) doll study, which found that African American preschoolers had a preference for White dolls. Since this study the idea that mainstream schooling promotes Whiteness and has a detrimental effect on Black students has been a mainstay of the literature (Cross, 1991).

Accordingly, Coard made a number of recommendations for changing the school system. He advocated amendments to the testing arrangements so that IQ scores were no longer used to judge Black children, the incorporation of Black history and culture in the curriculum, and the formal inclusion of Caribbean educationalists in devising school practice and reform. He argued that parents needed to be engaged in the process of schooling by visiting the schools, reading to the children, and making sure the school was acting in the best interests of the child. Coard's book is also practical, providing a question and answer section for parents on ESN and on children's rights to transfer out of the system. So although Coard presents a damning, and somewhat polemical, indictment of the mainstream school system, he does not believe it is completely beyond salvation. Key to the Black education movement has been a drive to reform the system to make it work for Black children (Grosvenor, 1997; John, 2006).

Importantly, however, alongside school reform Coard also advocated the development of Black supplementary schools. With regard especially to issues of Black identity and the teaching of Black history and culture, he argued that mainstream schools could not be trusted to develop a complete nor competent curriculum. The issue of identity and self-esteem was essential to the educational success of Black children. Coard argued that 'our children need to have a sense of identity, pride, and belonging' as tools to survive racism (*ibid.*: 39). As demonstrated below, self-esteem and pride in Blackness is essential to understanding the Black supplementary school movement.

Situating the movement in the broader issues of migration and settlement helps to illustrate how the African Caribbean community took up the issue of schooling in the mid-to late 1960s. Once the deficits and discrimination their children were facing in school became apparent, Black communities mobilized campaigns to hold the education authorities accountable and to reform the school system. Black supplementary schools must be seen as part of this movement, with a central aim being that Black students achieve in mainstream schooling.

Structure of the book
Resisting Racism is split according to two different research projects I carried out to write the book. The first section aims to explain the emergence of the movement and analyses the fundamental principles and tensions within Black supplementary schooling. Chapter 1 details the archival study carried out at the George Padmore Institute and the in-depth interviews I have used as a basis for Part One.

Blackness lies at the heart of the Black supplementary school movement, yet the academic theory of race delegitimizes collective movements based on race. Chapter 2 offers a critique of such theory of race and outlines the diverse and fluid conception of Blackness that is essential to Black supplementary education.

Though Black supplementary schools have much in common, there are differences in both organization and philosophy between the programmes. Chapter 3 explores the major cleavage in the movement, between 'official' and 'self-help' programmes, and looks at how they have different conceptions of the purpose of supplementary schooling and the role of the state.

As segments of the supplementary school movement have become increasingly accommodated into state educational provision, the lens through which educational inequality is viewed has shifted to the cultural deficit model of underachievement. Chapter 4 charts the individualizing of both racism and school success that reflects this shift.

Chapter 5 analyses the more radical challenge to the mainstream school system offered by the construction of African-centred education in the supplementary school movement. Though including calls for alternative curricula and independent schools, these approaches do not fundamentally challenge mainstream schooling, as they are ultimately based on the same view of success.

The second part of the book draws on an ethnographic study I conducted on one of the longest-running projects that I have called the 'Lumumba School'. Chapter 6 outlines the methodological approach to the study, while Chapter 7 is presented as a Research Diary, to allow the reader to gain a full understanding of the experience of teaching in a Black supplementary school. The theoretical discussions presented in Part One are used to explore the experiences in the Lumumba School in Part Two. Chapter 8 is used to draw out some of the key themes from the Lumumba study for discussion. Finally, the book brings together all of the strands of the research to discuss the implications and the prospects for the future of the Black supplementary school movement.

Part One

The Black supplementary
school movement

Chapter 1
Researching the movement

The book begins with an analysis of the emergence, forms of organization, and tensions within the Black supplementary school movement. The discussions that follow in Chapters 2 to 5 are based on a reading of the literature and on two research projects conducted for the book. This chapter outlines the archival study carried out at the George Padmore Institute into the emergence of the supplementary schools that arose out of the New Beacon bookshop and provides an historical context for the development of the wider movement. To get further insights into the principles and debates within Black supplementary schooling, interviews were conducted with a range of people involved in the Black supplementary school movement.

George Padmore Institute archival research

Central to understanding Black supplementary schools is situating the movement in the historical context of resistance to racism in education. It is therefore necessary to examine how projects emerged in the late 1960s and early 1970s. One of the earliest proponents of Black supplementary schooling was John La Rose, who also founded New Beacon Books in North London (Chevannes and Reeves, 1989). Alongside the publication and distribution of the largest collection of Black literature in the country, New Beacon was a hive of activity, drawing in writers and activists such as Bernard Coard and C.L.R. James, as well as building connections with organizations and movements, including the Caribbean Education and Community Workers Association (CECWA) and the Black Parents Movement (Alleyne, 2002). Supplementary schooling was a fundamental part of the package of resistance that emerged out of the period, and understanding how it was developed by the collective around New Beacon is instructive.

Alongside the activism of John La Rose and the New Beacon collective, one of their major successes was the foresight to guard the history of the movement. Important documents, minutes, notes, flyers, and the like were retained. The historical stewardship was formalized in 1991 with the opening of the George Padmore Institute, above the New Beacon bookshop. The Institute is home to an extensive archive of documents, including collections on the New Cross Massacre Campaign, the Black Parents Movement, and the Caribbean Artists Movement. The following section is based on the research of the Black Education Movement collection and of the archive, and also a selection from their collection from the Black Parents Movement. These represent only a small fraction of the archive. The analysis of documents is a key tool in social research to help develop understanding (Atkinson and Coffey, 2004) and here I explore how Black supplementary schooling emerged from the wider educational movement in the case of the New Beacon collective. The discussions, experiences, and actions that took place around New Beacon are not representative of the development of supplementary schools across the country, as each has emerged in its own given contexts. Also, the New Beacon case should not be viewed as foundational to the development of supplementary schooling. The particular importance of New Beacon is that they kept detailed records of how the movement emerged in their context and the principles and practice upon which it was founded. These can be used as a case study to explore the development of Black supplementary schooling. They draw out the debates, tensions, and principles upon which these specific programmes were founded, so help to explore the history, present, and future of the movement.

Anti-banding campaign

In 1969 Haringey Council put forward proposals to bring in a system of banding in primary schools, based on ability measured by IQ testing. There was widespread opposition to these proposals, with British, Caribbean, Greek, and socialist groups being central in forming a coalition of resistance. The campaign pulled no punches: parents threatened to boycott the schools if the proposals went through. A chord was struck across different communities: the parents' opposition was based not solely on the racist impact the changes would have but also on issues of class, testing, and parental choice. However, because of the disproportionate rates at which Black children were condemned to the bands of the educationally subnormal, the North London West Indian Association (NLWIA) launched their anti-banding campaign to highlight the assault on the Black community the proposals represented.

In the petition against the proposals, the NLWIA (1969b: 1) wrote in strong terms that the council would not be allowed to use their children as 'racial scapegoats'. In a leaflet the NLWIA (1969a: 1) promised to fight the proposals, as 'no price will be too high to pay for the future of our children and theirs after them'. For the NLWIA the banding proposals were another attack based on the exclusionary and dangerous views about the education of immigrant children. A leaked document written for the council known as the Doulton Report was a typical example.

A.J.F Doulton, headteacher of a fee-paying school, was, ironically, commissioned to write a report on Haringey comprehensives (Doulton, 1969). The NLWIA was incensed by Doulton's approach to the 'problem' of the number of Caribbean immigrants who would be in the school system. He asserted that:

> On a rough calculation about half the immigrants will be West Indians at 7 of the 11 schools, the significance of this being the general recognition that their IQs work out below their English contemporaries. Thus academic standards will be lower in schools where they form a large group.
>
> (Doulton, 1969: 3)

Doulton argued that, because of the perceived deficits in their intelligence, Caribbean students must be dispersed so as not to weaken certain schools and thus 'reinforce divisions' (*ibid.*: 4). The Doulton Report was the only piece of documentation from the council at the time that openly subscribed to the view that African Caribbean students were less intelligent than their British counterparts. The NLWIA argued, however, that the report revealed the true motivation for the council's plans for banding and the dispersal of African Caribbean children in the school system. The official report from the London Borough of Haringey published in 1969 was a sanitized version of Doulton's report as it made clear that the borough did not want to see a large concentration of immigrants in any one school. Consequently, the racist nature of the proposals was at the forefront of the NLWIA campaign. One of its flyers warned that 'our children are threatened', and proclaimed that the council had declared 'a war against Black people's children' (NLWIA, nd: 1).

Campaigns to change the mainstream

The NLWIA's responses to the banding proposals and the Doulton Report sought primarily to change how the schools worked and reduce the inequalities in the system. The main objection was to the use of IQ tests, as these were culturally biased against Caribbean children. However, the NLWIA also used the anti-banding issue to draw attention to other problems affecting Black children in schools. The NLWIA (1969a: 2) released a number of proposals for the education of Black children in Britain. These included appointing Caribbean teachers, who were 'emotionally and culturally attuned' to the children; providing courses for parents to inform them of school changes; providing nursery places; and incorporating community groups into the management of schools.

Black mobilization around New Beacon emphasized the need to change mainstream schools and their relationship with the Black community. The Black Parents Movement (BPM) that originated in 1975 is characteristic. Following the 'violent attack by the Hornsey police in North London on a Black school student', a group of concerned parents and community members worked together to hold the police force accountable for their assault (BPM, nd: 2). After the resolution of the initial case the BPM did not disband but continued in their 'struggles with the police, courts, and over education, schooling, housing, and employment' (BPM, nd: 2).

The BPM spread to other parts of the country, most notably Manchester, and was engaged in large-scale campaigns such as protests over the New Cross Massacre, and the National Day of Action (Alleyne, 2002). The Black Youth Movement (originally the Black Students Movement) arose out of the same incident that led to the creation of the BPM. It too was involved in campaigns against police harassment and efforts to change education. These groups campaigned to hold mainstream institutions accountable for their actions.

The George Padmore archive has a section dedicated to the BPM and this allows exploration of the extent and importance of the movement. Detailed exploration is beyond the scope of this work, but it is important to understand the background and context in which Black supplementary schools emerged. Supplementary schools were very much part of a wider movement to hold the mainstream school system to account for its failings towards Black children. As the Black Students Movement (1978: 1) explained:

> During the 60s black parents in Haringey were constantly struggling for better education for their children. An aspect of this struggle was the formation of black supplementary schools.

Black education

Out of the anti-banding campaign, alongside the campaigns for reform of the school system, arose a call for the development of suitable education for African Caribbean children. The West Indian Standing Conference (1970: 2) agreed to look into the provision of extra schooling for Caribbean children who had been 'left out in the cold'. In June 1970 the NLWIA and those around New Beacon formed a new organization called the Caribbean Educationists Association, dedicated to the 'growing threat to the education of the Black child in Britain' (CEA, 1970: 1). After much discussion and several name changes the organization eventually became the Caribbean Education and Community Workers Association (CECWA), bringing together people in the community who were passionate about education. Its constitution declares its aims to promote links to Caribbean culture, form study groups concerning the history and culture of Black people, and, importantly, to:

> initiate and promote the establishment of Supplementary Education Schemes through which West Indian children can be provided with an unbiased account of the history of black people, with special reference to the development of communities in the West Indies.
> (CECWA, nd: 1)

CECWA was interested in influencing mainstream schooling and saw Black supplementary schooling as one platform through which inequities in the school system, particularly in the curriculum, could be challenged. Black supplementary schools represent spaces created and controlled by Black communities, so they allow activists power that they may lack when campaigning for mainstream reform. However, they should not be considered separate from the campaigns that sought to change the mainstream schools.

After decades of campaigning for influence on mainstream schooling, Gus John, a notable Black educational activist in Britain, made the following comments at a National Association of Multicultural Education conference:

> We seem to spend so much time talking to, with, or about white people, or posturing for their benefit on matters to do with race and anti-racism; the whole system has got us so caught up in this activity ... If we were to put half the time into learning to talk with and listen to one another in free, open, and democratic discourse that we put into leading the thinking of white folk, or operating the structures into which we are incorporated on the race ticket, our struggle will be considerably more advanced.
> (John, 1987: 6)

Campaigning to change the school system will to some extent always be framed by those who control the system. The power relations are marked by the need to convince local authorities or the government to change their minds and behaviour, to legislate for the inclusion of Black children in education. This means that activism must engage with those in power through methods and language they understand. One of the major objections to more radical conceptions of Black politics and the idea of Black independent organizations has been the fear of alienating the very White people who have the power to bring about changes to the system (King, 1969). John is expressing frustration that in order to work within the system, activists were compelled to 'posture' and follow the rules of the game as defined by those in power and the people with this power, especially early in the Black education movement, were White.

Although an increasing number of Black and Asian people have gained access to jobs and advancement in mainstream institutions, this does not necessarily change the nature of this situation. The problem was not simply that those running the institutions were White and that this meant that their lack of understanding of the Black community had to be taken into account. The issue was, and remains, that the institutions themselves are founded on principles based on Whiteness as the norm (Henry, 2007). This determines, for example, the way that race and racism are understood (explored in Chapter 2), or the composition of the school curriculum. Those who work in and for mainstream institutions adopt positions that are framed by Whiteness. John's frustration is not because of having to talk to White people *per se*, but because of the constant need for him to speak and act in ways defined by hegemonic Whiteness. The reality that there are now Black and Asian people in mainstream positions of power and influence does not change this dynamic if the fundamental principles of the institution remain products of this Whiteness. As the BPM (nd: 3) explain: 'We believe that state-sponsored organizations such as the CRE (Commission for Racial Equality) have existed and still exist to handicap the independent Black movement.' Therefore, even state organizations that were specifically set up to deal with problems of racism (such as the CRE), and hired significant numbers of Black and Asians to do so, were criticized for perpetuating hegemonic Whiteness.

Whiteness and its influence over Black educational movements was, and remains, a central issue. At the founding of the BPM there was a big debate about whether the White parent of a Black child could join the organization. Some in the organization felt that a White 'parent had a natural interest in joining with black parents to fight in their children's interests because their children were regarded in this society as black' (BPM, 1978: 1). White people were initially allowed to join the organization only if they were in a relationship with a BPM member. However, this was not to be seen as a 'soft option', as 'they would have to agree to work in the White community on issues similar to those taken up by the BPM' (*ibid.*: 2).

The issue of White membership was important, as it went to the core of what it meant to be a Black organization. It was seen as essential that the space remained Black-controlled in order to be a voice for those in the community. The centrality of the issue is highlighted by the dispute between the founding branch of the BPM in Haringey and the one set up later in Hackney, which broke down over the membership of Whites in the Hackney branch. The lack of discussion and communication over the issue caused the

Hackney section to be dissolved as part of the BPM. Eventually the BPM decided not to allow the membership of White parents in the organization but to limit to two categories those who could join: namely any Black parent and any 'Black persons who [were] not parents but [were] otherwise acceptable to the membership' (*ibid.*: 2). Ultimately, the importance of it being a Black-controlled space was seen as paramount.

The Black supplementary school movement also saw the creation of a Black-controlled space of education as essential. Success in the mainstream was fundamental to the work of the programmes, but it was also seen as necessary to produce an education for Black children. A comment from the floor at the Supplementary Schools Conference (1987: 7) hosted by the Inner London Education Authority encapsulated the feeling that supplementary schools needed to build an education that could create 'understanding, self-awareness, and self confidence in our [Black] children which will be a source of strength for them in facing the outside world'. Another comment from the conference highlights the lack of faith in the ability of mainstream provision to produce such an education: a questioner from the floor asked 'how long are we going to go on to allow our enemies to educate our children to become [their] servants?' (*ibid.*: 7). This comment illustrates a particularly cynical view of the purpose of mainstream schooling and is not necessarily a widespread position. However, it does reflect how education that is produced in schooling can be seen as inadequate for Black children. While the majority of those in the Black supplementary school movement would not see the issue in such absolute terms, with Whites as the enemy, the emphasis remains on providing a Black curriculum, controlled by Black organizations, from which the children can benefit.

The George Padmore and Albertina Sylvester schools

The two Black supplementary schools that emerged out of New Beacon were named George Padmore and Albertina Sylvester. Both started in 1969 and New Beacon founder John La Rose (1976: 1) explained the origins of the programmes:

> Our initial inspiration for beginning our work was our recognition that the state schools were failing most black students in providing a knowledge of and understanding of our black history and culture as well as the basic three Rs.

The projects were run out of the homes of their founders (John La Rose and Albertina Sylvester, respectively) and in this sense they capture the early spirit of the movement. In response to their concerns about racism in the school system, many parents took matters into their own hands and began providing extra tuition for the children and friends, when and where they could, and this often meant in their homes on a Saturday (Mirza and Reay, 2000). Not all programmes were run on Saturday: the George Padmore School, for example, was held on week nights. The school began with five children on the books and by 1972 had grown to the point of needing three regular teachers. The teaching was split into different age groups: years 1–3 and years 4–6, and averaged 12–14 students per group. The Albertina Sylvester School was run on a Saturday and averaged around 10 children each week, with a maximum of 14 by 1972.

The dedication that has gone into Black supplementary schooling is evident in the way people in the community opened up their homes in the evenings and weekends to large numbers of children. As is apparent throughout the book, this commitment is the driving force of the movement.

After running as separate projects until 1975, the George Padmore and Albertina Sylvester schools merged into one supplementary school, along with two other projects in the area, the George Washington Carver and Pamela Brown schools. It was felt that more comprehensive provision would be possible in the merged schools, which had together taught between 40 and 50 children each term.

The aim was to buy premises and move the projects from the teachers' houses. Coordination of this kind has unfortunately not characterized the Black supplementary school movement, with projects tending to remain isolated even when in the same neighbourhoods (Best, 1990). The vision that informed the collective of the four schools was, however, to take the organization of the movement to another level and to provide comprehensive provision for the community. The attempt to raise funds for this expansion of supplementary school provision paints a picture of the fundamental underpinning of the movement.

Funding and curriculum

When they originally opened, both the George Padmore and Albertina Sylvester schools charged no fee to the parents who brought their children, as the wish was not to turn away people who could not afford a fee. This highlights the small-scale voluntary project origins, often located in organizers' homes – it also meant that there were few overheads. However, as the projects grew they had to charge nominal fees for attendance to make them sustainable. When the projects began to expand, especially after the merger and the plans to relocate to dedicated accommodation, the supplementary schools needed to find funding. They looked primarily to two sources and these have defined how the movement has developed.

The first source of potential funding was the state. Applications were made and letters written to various levels of local and national government and organizations including the Haringey Community Development Unit and the Urban Aid grant programme. The most successful application was to the Institute of Race Relations, which pledged £2,000 for the organization towards purchasing premises. The role of state funding has been a contentious one throughout the history of supplementary schools. That the George Padmore and Albertina Sylvester schools were prepared to apply for state funding demonstrates that they saw the supply of supplementary schooling as the responsibility of the state. As is discussed in Chapter 3, whether or not state support for the projects was welcome was determined by the position a supplementary school took on the role of mainstream education.

The second source of potential funding was the Black-led churches, which have played a central organizing role within the African Caribbean community and remain one of the few longstanding, financially viable community organizations (Hylton, 1999). The influence of the church is keenly felt within the community. This was acknowledged by Jocelyn Barrow, a key member of the early CECWA, who declared that 'no other group or individual among us has the authority of the black churchman' (WIE, nd: 8). It is no surprise that the supplementary school movement looked to the Black-led churches for support, and the George Padmore and Albertina Sylvester schools wrote to several. The largest pledge of support for the purchase of a building came from the British Council of Churches, who offered £3,000. Churches also offered support in the form of the use of church premises to run occasional sessions for the expanded programmes, which is a common feature of Black supplementary schooling (see Chapter 3). That the schools emerging from New Beacon accepted funds from both the state and Black-led churches confirms that the projects were working alongside and not presenting radical challenges to the system of schooling. This collaborative stance has implications for the curriculum of Black supplementary schools.

Instruction in the basic academic subjects was a central part of the work carried out in the George Padmore and Albertina Sylvester schools and has been a hallmark of the movement (Stone, 1981). The George Padmore Institute archive contains a number of maths and English worksheets completed by students that could have been found in any mainstream school at the time. The aim was clearly to help the students to succeed using the tools and assessment strategies they would encounter in mainstream education.

Alongside this extension of mainstream schooling, Black education was developed by the supplementary school programmes.

Attention was paid to the role of history and the contemporary Caribbean in the schools. Caribbean folklore, literature, and history were a strong focus – an attempt to make up for the deficit in the mainstream curriculum. Passing on this cultural legacy was seen as important to developing the pride that Coard had claimed was lacking among Black schoolchildren, and the George Padmore School exposed the students to radical and alternative takes on the political situation facing Black people.

Reading comprehension was a typical exercise in the supplementary schools and featured work by, for example, Marcus Garvey; information about the slave rebellion of Nat Turner; and the writings of Black Panthers such as George Jackson. These supplementary school programmes clearly presented curriculum material that challenged mainstream concepts and practices. At the same time, however, the projects were dedicated to achieving success for the students in mainstream schools and were committed to working with the state educational bodies at local and national level. These apparent contradictions, discussed in Chapter 3, go to the core of the Black supplementary school movement.

Interview study

The purpose of the interview study was to understand how Black supplementary schools programmes are organized and to comprehend their underpinning philosophies. Accordingly, I targeted as interviewees those who had founded or led projects. This allowed for a broad range of supplementary schools to be investigated.

I interviewed 14 people, seven men and seven women, who were involved in running various Black supplementary projects. I recruited them on an opportunity sample basis, starting with my contacts and then through word of mouth. The directory of Nia Imara from the National Association of Black Supplementary Schools was essential in recruiting participants. Three people who ran supplementary schools whom I contacted declined to be in the study. I recruited participants from different types of supplementary schools. The participants were involved in the movement in a variety of ways, as described below. All have been given pseudonyms:

> *Menelik* directed a long-running programme on a self-help basis, based in a radical political organization.
> *Gloria* was a mainstream teacher who taught in a Saturday school and arranged summer school projects.

Kwame founded the summer school programme with a community group.

Jason organized a Saturday school project linked to a local cultural association.

Errol was part of a national organization linked to a church group.

Rose organized a weekend supplementary school that was also linked to a church.

Henry taught at *Rose*'s project.

Angela ran a supplementary evening school in the 1980s.

Clive was the coordinator of a Saturday school until 2005.

Lorraine had been involved in setting up supplementary schools since the 1990s and was interested in setting up full-time independent schools.

Carlton ran a supplementary school located in a Black-led church.

Sonia had played a part in the movement for over 20 years.

Palsent was involved in the running of a supplementary school that started in the 1970s.

Sarah worked for a university and organized a Saturday school for African Caribbean boys as part of the widening participation agenda.

All of the participants were Black except for Sarah. She was White and worked on a Black supplementary school project that was one of various initiatives organized by her university for a range of communities and target groups.

Kwame, Clive, Angela, Sonia, and Lorraine were not actively involved in supplementary projects at the time I interviewed them. Clive's project stopped in 2005 but the intention was for it to start again in the future. Kwame ended his work with the summer school project he founded but was looking to start another. Angela founded a supplementary evening school in the late 1970s and had not been involved in supplementary schools since it closed. Sonia had recently stopped being part of the movement after 20 years. Interviews with those connected with the movement in past decades give this book its important historical perspective. Lorraine had moved on from supplementary schools and was now trying to establish independent schools.

In addition, there were two interviewees who had other attachments to the movement: Nia Imara, who set up the National Association of Black Supplementary Schools, and Pascale Vassie from an organization called ContinYou, which runs an accreditation scheme for supplementary schools. Both of their organizations came up frequently in the interviews with the others and they made a unique contribution to my research. They were not given pseudonyms because discussions about their organizations were helpful to this book.

The interview process
All of the interviews were one to one except for Rose and Henry, who were interviewed together, simply because both were present when I arrived for the interview. It turned out to be advantageous, as they added to the interpretive process by questioning, supporting, and challenging each other's statements. Interviews were semi-structured and lasted between an hour and 90 minutes. Some of the interviews were conducted over the telephone because of distance.

The questions were focused around seven main topics (for the full interview schedule, see Appendix):

- *Organization of the schools*: how they were started, number of children and teachers, etc.
- *Curriculum*: what was taught in the supplementary projects.
- *Funding*: where they drew financial support.
- *Philosophy*: the ideology and ethos behind the school.
- *Blackness*: what the term meant to participants.
- *Role of the church*: importance of Black-led churches to the functioning of the school.
- *Future*: what next for Black supplementary schools?

The interviews were conducted using an interpretive approach, and the interview schedule was used to guide the conversation in preference to asking set questions in a predetermined order. The participants were encouraged to shape the conversation and this led to a wealth of insights and discussions.

Conclusion
Neither the archival nor the interview study is meant to stand as representative of the experiences of the entire Black supplementary school movement in Britain. However, the range of sources and interviewees researched does allow for a comprehensive analysis of the fundamental principles, tensions, and debates that have emerged in the movement overall. The following four chapters are an exploration of these issues. They draw on the archival data, interview transcripts, and literature on Black supplementary schools.

Chapter 2
The role of Blackness

The embrace of Blackness in the Black supplementary school movement runs contrary to much theory on race within academia. In Britain race has largely been abandoned as a meaningful organizational category and has been relegated to 'scare quotes' (Alexander, 2002). This chapter explains that the delegitimization of race in academic theory is due to three main flaws. The first is the belief that race, and therefore Blackness, is a concept solely created by the majority society in the West, in order to exploit those with darker skins. Second, the focus on *political blackness*, and its strategic essentialism on non-Whites in theoretical and practical terms; and third, the postmodern turn that emphasizes de-essentialized, fluid, fractured identities which signal the end of race (Gilroy, 1998). The chapter explores how these theoretical flaws undermine the concept of Blackness based in African ancestry. However, this concept is essential to the organization of the Black community, and supplementary schooling is emblematic of such endeavours.

Academic constructions of race
The Marxist account of race is dominant within academia in terms of racial formation. Objections to the utility of race are often based on the belief that Europeans created the concept in order to exploit the dark masses of the world (Cole, 2003; Miles and Brown, 2003). Therefore race, and not simply racism, is a form of capitalist oppression and there is no other basis to the category than the social construction of distinct groups in order for those of European descent to dominate. From this perspective, to *see* race is to *be* racist. From a Marxist point of view the only form of politics that can liberate society is class-based and therefore organizing around racial collectivity obscures the shared struggle of the 'workers of the world' (Robinson, 1983).

Though Marxism is in many ways a critique of mainstream academic positions, on the issue of racial categorizations there is important convergence. As with Marxism, racism is at the periphery rather than at the centre of the liberal view of society (Bell, 1992; Peller, 1995). 'Racialization' is a commonly used term in academia, which shows the level of acceptance of the Marxist formation of racial categories. Where the liberal view does differ is that, for liberals, society has changed fundamentally since enslavement. Racism has moved to the margins, along with gender, sexuality, and disability (Peller,

1995). From a liberal standpoint the nature of these inequalities is the same. All largely revolve around changing attitudes so as to address the inequalities produced. The dissolution of the Commission for Racial Equality and its incorporation into the Equality and Human Rights Commission in the UK in 2006 illustrates how the state conceives of inequalities in this model (Hirsh, 2009). It is individuals in society who are racist, according to this view, and they need to be targeted. In a modern society, phenotypical differences are meaningless and the ultimate goal of certain visions of liberalism is a colour-blind society where people are judged 'not by the colour of their skin but the content of their personality' (King, 1963: np). Again, notice that to *see* race is to *be* racist. The justification here is slightly different, however, from that which emanates from a Marxist standpoint.

To see race, from a liberal perspective, is to be racist because racial differences are a concept from the past and so colour blindness is the appropriate rational, enlightened, liberal position, and to recognize different races is a throwback to a backward age (Crenshaw, 1995). What defines the liberal position is the idea of progressing away from pre- and counter-modern understandings towards a more open society. The narrative of the banishment of race and racism is key in demonstrating this progress: contemporary liberal society is said to be progressive because it has left racial explanations in the past.

Discrimination against vs. discrimination between

The justification for the 'to see race is to be racist' argument is the history of phrenology and race science, which was used to defend all kinds of inequality. The horrors of the Nazi death camps brought home (perhaps in ways that enslavement and colonialism could not) the consequences of Western racial categorizations (Leach, 2005). Race as biology and as being deterministic of ability was used as the basis for genocide, and it was seen as necessary that these concepts were all swept away. However, dismissing alternative concepts of race is premature and misses the distinction between discrimination *against* and discrimination *between* (Younge, 1999).

Racism is fundamentally based on discrimination *against*. Different races are earmarked and placed into a hierarchy founded on perceived phenotypical differences. Discrimination *between*, however, is the process of categorizing difference based on a set criterion. That discrimination between automatically leads to discrimination against is a fallacy. In the case of racism, that Europeans discerned different races and formed a hierarchy with themselves at the pinnacle does not mean that this is the only consequence of seeing race (Niro, 2003). It is well documented that those whom Europeans encountered on their travels also categorized people on the basis of phenotypical differences – for instance, the Native Americans (Kilcup, 2000) and Southern Africans (Mutwa, 1998). The difference between these categorizations is that in America the native population embraced the settlers, and in parts of Africa, Whites were welcomed and trade links were formed. In return the native populations suffered genocide, enslavement, and colonialism in their encounters with Whites. Just because the West has used difference to dominate, control, and slaughter does not make difference itself the problem.

When interviewed, Angela exemplified this necessary distinction:

> You've got to acknowledge that we're not all same, they accept that a man and woman are different, why don't you accept then that you have people who are you know, their parents came originally say from the Caribbean, or came from India, or came from Africa, if you accept that then you've got to see there's a history behind the way those people are thinking as well as the communication and um, other things that they have with their parents.

Angela is arguing that it is the histories of various people that make us different. To see differences between different groups is not to reify and racialize, but simply to acknowledge what exists. To note that those of African ancestry have similar phenotypical features and cultures broadly based on the same foundation is not only acceptable, it is desirable. It is only when these differences are used to 'denigrate' those who are different that problems occur. In order to understand Angela's remarks, it is crucial to grasp that this acceptance of difference is essential if we are to understand society and act to resist racism.

A fundamental error in Western research is to base the concept of race entirely on how the West has viewed race. Alternate understandings of the concepts are silenced and race is abandoned as an analytic and practical organizing tool. In light of the thorough and numerous critiques of Eurocentrism by various postcolonial and critical scholars (Gran, 1996; Said, 2003), this should come as no surprise. Historically, one of the foundational problems of knowledge produced in the West is Eurocentrism and a colonial universality (Hall, 2007). In other words, because the West got it wrong on race, the concept *itself* must be the problem and not the Western interpretation. The Western understanding of race is certainly the dominant one, but that does not make it the correct one. There are ways to see race that are both progressive and necessary. The Black supplementary school movement has used constructions of Blackness that have long traditions of both explaining society and organizing to change it. To understand how these constructions have impacted on the supplementary school movement it is necessary to trace the emergence of the term 'Black' and its use in the British context.

From Negro to Black

Blackness is not simply a creation by Europeans who assigned biological attributes on the basis of colour. For Black people, the basis of their identity was never biological or phenotypical but instead historical, cultural, and experiential (Asante, 2003). An African identity arose from contact with other cultures with distinct bases. Blackness becomes important in the Western context, in which millions of Africans were forcibly removed from the continent and enslaved. A central process during enslavement was to both dehumanize and deAfricanize the enslaved so as to pacify and thus control them. Much of the success of the Haitian revolution has been attributed to the high number of the enslaved on the island who had been born in Africa, which meant there was no accommodation to slave society and they maintained a vibrant African culture and identity in the population (James, 1938). Africaness was purposefully beaten out of the enslaved populations in the West and with the successive generations born outside of the continent the connections to Africa diminished. Since enslavement, there remains a large population with African ancestry in the West and the terms used to describe this and connect back to the people of Africa have varied in different times and places. 'Negro', 'Coloured', 'Black', 'Afro-Caribbean', 'African' have all been popular at one time and place or another (Martin, 1991).

What is often overlooked is that the terminology used is neither random nor coincidental but demarcates a political progression in identity for those of African ancestry. Far from being legislated by the wider society, the progression from 'Nigger' to 'African', via 'Black', is the result of an ideological struggle by the Black community for pride and independence. The term 'Black', which is now taken for granted, is relatively recent and was hard fought for. Menelik attested to this when he spoke about being unable to use 'African' in the name of their political group in the 1960s:

> Because people them days wouldn't accept the word African much less Black, you get punched in the face call somebody Black, so people was known as Negroes and Coloured.

Black as an identity was popularized in the West by people such as Malcolm X and later the Black Power movement in the United States in the 1970s (Carmichael and Hamilton, 1969). Decades before this, Marcus Garvey, while still using the term 'Negro', called for racial pride, saying, 'the black skin is not a symbol of shame but a glorious symbol of greatness' (Cronon, 1969: 4). The idea was to overcome the negative ascriptions of the dominant society and rally round Blackness, i.e. our common descent from Africa. The next step was to define ourselves not as Negroes or Coloureds but as Black. Malcolm X explains this development by contrasting the Negro and Black revolutions (X, 1971). The Negro revolution was led by people who did not know themselves or their history and were trying to impress White society, whereas the Black revolution is led by those who have transcended and understood their history, and who are determined to become free, independent of White society. Stokely Carmichael (1971: 114) argued that 'every Negro is a potential Black man'.

Becoming Black was a development that extended beyond the realm of politics. William Cross (1971) was a social psychologist who published a paper entitled 'The Negro to Black Conversion Experience' and founded the field of Black Racial Identity. In his paper he charted the development from being in a Negro state, in a White reference frame, to literally *becoming* Black and seeing the world from a different perspective. From being in the 'pre-encounter' Negro identity, a person could have an 'encounter' that would switch them on to their Blackness. The assassination of Martin Luther King, for example, was said to trigger an 'immersion/emersion' phase where a person engaged only in Black or Afrocentric experiences. Eventually the final transition would be a move to the 'internalization-committed' identity, where the Black person devoted themselves to the uplift of their people.

The same development occurred in the UK, as Menelik indicates. Black was followed by Afro and then African. This is extremely important to the understanding of Blackness because it shows how inextricably linked it is to African ancestry. Garvey was a Jamaican who toured the Caribbean and Americas in the early twentieth century, advocating a return to Africa (Garvey, 1923). Though he never travelled to the continent, his writings were an inspiration to African leaders such as Kwame Nkrumah, Jomo Kenyatta, and Julius Nyere (Nkrumah, 1963; Walvin, 2001). Malcolm X founded the Organization of Afro-American Unity, in the West, after travelling extensively through the African continent talking to the leaders of many countries (X, 1970). The term 'Black' is used to connect those people who are displaced back to Africa. This is why 'Afro' and 'African' were the logical next steps in identification.

West Indian to Black

To understand the emergence of Blackness as an organizing category in the British context, the concept must be framed in terms of migration. As we

The role of Blackness

saw in Chapter 1, when people from the Caribbean migrated to Britain they did so as West Indians, maintaining strong roots to their home countries and planning to return. It was only when the character of this migration turned to settlement that the community began to see itself as British, but with the qualifier of being Black. The absence of the use of 'Black' for the early migrants relates also to the situation and terminology used in the Caribbean islands at the time of migration. As Stuart Hall (1991: 53) recounts:

> Until I left [Jamaica], though I suppose 98 per cent of the Jamaican population is either Black or colored in one way or another, I had never ever heard anybody either call themselves, or refer to anybody else, as 'Black'. Never. I heard a thousand other words. My grandmother could differentiate about fifteen different shades between light brown and dark brown.

Although 'Black' was not used in the Caribbean before the 1960s, this does not indicate that the phenomenon of Blackness occurred solely in relation to experiences in Britain. Hall notes that the first time he heard the term 'Black' was 'in the wake of the Civil Rights Movement, in the wake of the decolonization and nationalistic struggles' (*ibid.*: 54). This is testament to the history of the term; 'Black' was not widely adopted by any population until the politics of resistance that embraced the term were developed in the mid- to late 1960s. The Caribbean also experienced this embrace of Blackness, and the government of Jamaica, for example, made much effort to deter its population from following Black Power politics (Nettleford, 1970). Though Blackness exists in the Caribbean, it takes on a salient role for migrant communities in the UK.

As Hall points out, when the majority of the population is Black, difference is understood in other terms. Becoming a minority of colour, once in Britain, Blackness becomes much more noticeable and important. Crucially this does not mean that people became Black when they arrived in Britain. The 98 per cent of the population to which Hall refers were Black in Jamaica, but their Blackness was not as salient a feature in terms of conceptualizing their differences. The same can be said for Black Africans, where again the concept of Black is not necessarily mobilized. In the African context, connection of Blackness is embodied in the term 'Africanism' (Mandela, 1996).

Minority status and experiences of racism in Britain led to resistance from the community that became framed in Blackness. At the beginning of the supplementary school movement this resistance was tied strongly to a West Indian identity. The early literature and meetings were organized by West Indian or Caribbean groups and their defence of 'West Indian history, culture, customs, and traditions' (WISC, 1970: 3). Reading the highly West Indian-centric early literature it is possible to conclude that the supplementary school movement is not about Blackness but rather about Caribbean resistance to racism in education. However, this would be a mistake, as the concept of West Indian was at the outset being conflated with the concept of Blackness. For instance, at the first meeting of the Caribbean Educationists Association (CEA, 1970: 3), the organization declared that 'it was important to note that this weekend seminar was open only to Black people. We feel that the time has come when we, as West Indians, must talk with ourselves.' What is clear from this statement is that, in this context, the conceptions of West Indian and Black are not separate. West Indians are seen as being Black people, which is defined as being of African ancestry. At the same conference, CEA (*ibid.*: 3) commented on the 'increasing Black consciousness among West Indians'. For Caribbeans in the UK there was a process of becoming Black and adopting the political commitment to people of African ancestry.

African ancestry as the root of Blackness was a universal theme among those I interviewed, be it Clive talking about Black societies, or Angela constantly referencing South African, Caribbean, and American Black people. Talking in terms of the Diaspora was a very strong theme on which the participants drew. Errol explained how Blackness was tied to his African ancestry and captured the spirit of Black empowerment in his work in supplementary schools using Black pride to overcome the negative representations of Black people:

> You get the image of Black people, our history started in slavery, you forget all of the African kingdoms and the like ... and so we don't want our young people to recognize, or to believe that we were just slaves and we're always slaves and we're gonna be slaves, and gonna be impoverished. That's not the case at all, and we actively encourage them to travel to see Black people in the Caribbean, in Africa, doing, go to Africa, and see, Black people aren't scratching around with dirt with flies in their eyes ... I'd say I love being Black, I mean I just, I love it, I love our culture, I love our food, I love our language, I'll even love some of the things that aren't brilliant, I love that as well, some of it makes me laugh, some of it makes me cry, but I love being Black.

The predominance of Caribbean migrants and their descendants in the supplementary movement and in the construction of Blackness in Britain more generally raises the important issue of how those of direct African descent fit into this construction of Black.

Blackness and Africans

During the interviews with my participants, it was not always clear whether they were including those of Black African descent when they referred to Black people and the community and culture, or solely those from the Caribbean. The distinctly Caribbean nature of the movement could indicate a separation of African and Caribbean populations in Britain, a notion that challenges the idea of a cohesive Blackness based on African ancestry. There are certainly differences between those who hail from the African continent and those from the Caribbean, and there have been tensions among the communities (Sudbury, 2001). There has been a tendency to see Africans as model minorities who succeed in school and society whereas the Caribbean population is associated with poor educational attainment, unemployment, and crime. This view has not only been held by White society and is a significant cause of the friction that has existed between the communities in the past. Due to the process of de-Africanization that took place within slavery, the African roots of Black people in the Caribbean have not always been cherished by Black communities.

The role that fellow Africans played in the trade of those taken to the Caribbean has been another source of contention, so it is impossible to paint a picture of an idyllic and harmonious connection between the communities since they settled in Britain. However, the Black supplementary school movement is largely free of such unwelcome community dynamics of Black Britain. The movement rests on a conception of Blackness that rejects all colonial readings and unites the people of African ancestry into a common collective and resistance. Consequently, the largely Caribbean movement is predicated on a restoration of Black pride explicitly tied to the continent of Africa.

Enslavement for Caribbeans is the trauma through which our place in the West is understood. This obviously does not translate in the same way to the experience of those who remained on the continent. However, Africa is essential in the redemption of Blackness. As Menelik declared, 'There were great civilizations in Africa, and Black history didn't just start at slavery.' There is a purposeful attempt to connect back to Africa in understanding Blackness. Therefore, although Black in the supplementary school movement has been predominantly defined by Black people of Caribbean descent, and hence it is framed in terms of the legacy of enslavement, this does not exclude those of African descent in Britain. I argue that though African immigrants to the UK do not share the narrative of the enslaved, they are filtered into society through the framework developed through interactions with and the history of Caribbean migrants.

The African presence in Britain can be traced back to the days of the Roman Empire, through to the sixteenth and seventeenth centuries, when enslaved Africans were brought to the country, and then to the small communities that arose in port cities such as Cardiff in the early twentieth century (Scobie, 1972). However, unlike migration from the Caribbean, there has been no particular period of mass migration of Africans from Africa, and the community has expanded only since the late 1970s. Consequently, Blackness in Britain was initially defined by the impact of the mass migration of Caribbeans, and the initial period of resistance against racism in education and society was led and framed by the Caribbean and Asian communities who had settled in larger numbers. This is not to say that there were no Africans involved in resistance or experiencing racism but the dominant Black experience was the Caribbean one and this framed how Blackness has been understood. Africans cannot be expected to fold neatly into the categorization of Black, especially considering the strongly Caribbean framing of the concept in the British context. However, there is evidence to suggest that as African settlement has progressed and there are now more people identifying as African rather than Caribbean (ONS, 2011), society is witnessing a conversion of African and African Caribbean into a Black British position in terms of both oppression and culture.

In the 1990s African students significantly outperformed Caribbeans, but recently the gap in educational attainment between the two groups has shrunk, with Africans trending downwards (DfE, 2007). The idea of the African school student as the model minority has far less purchase than in previous decades. It is unfortunate that in this convergence in the position of Black Britons, low educational achievement appears to be a constant, though this may speak to the power of the racial inequities in the school system and make the case for the continuance of the Black supplementary school movement.

More important than the convergence of inequalities is the development of a Black British culture that includes Africans. Successive generations of Africans and Caribbeans have combined to create a distinctive Black British cultural form, related to, but outside, the continental distinctions (Henry, 2006). With the advent of more British-born Black people, the African/Caribbean divide has lessened. Although all of the people I interviewed for this study were of Caribbean descent, they made a conscious effort to construct a Black identity that connected back to Africa. It should also be recognized that in London, a bigger Black African community has been involved in the movement for decades.

The pitfalls of political blackness

Political blackness attempts to unify all those in society who are victims of racism. All who are not White come under the term 'politically black', and are called to fight against their collective oppression (Sudbury, 2001). Embracing a politically black identity is done strategically to battle discrimination.

The central concept of non-White unity against oppression is also a feature of anti-racist movements in countries such as the United States and South Africa. In the USA the equivalent term is 'people of colour', which has a long history. South Africa, in its fight against apartheid, is perhaps the best example of the power of the concept of political blackness.

The horrors of apartheid and the consequences of such a racially hierarchical system have been well documented (Tutu, 2000). Many groups in South Africa fought against the system; these included the Pan African Congress, the South African Indian Congress, class-based groups such as the Communist Party, and tribal groupings, for instance, the Zulu Inkatha Freedom Party (Mandela, 1996). However, the group that eventually led South Africa out of apartheid was the African National Congress (ANC), a multi-racial party that embraced principles of political blackness. Uniting the different groups and bringing in sympathetic Whites was central to the victory of the ANC. Even Steve Biko's (1978) more radical Black Consciousness Movement (BCM) embraced a form of political blackness, being open to those categorized as Indians and Coloureds.

However, the coalition of political blackness in South Africa was based on the pragmatic alliance of different groups acting together. The ANC, though multi-racial, was founded and led mainly by Black Africans and this was essential to its identity. Mandela (1996) recalls the fears that the ANC would be co-opted by Whites, Indians, or Coloureds. The ANC began as an Africanist party and its legitimacy is taken from it being the voice of the Black majority. During the fight against apartheid the ANC connected with other groups to form the Congress Alliance, but this was made up of separate groups coming together because of a common goal.

Pragmatic alliances between groups in the UK developed to fight racial discrimination. For example, there has been cooperation between Black and Asian workers and groups such as the West Indian Standing Conference and the Indian Workers Association (Shukra, 1998). This history of ethnic groups collaborating must not be underestimated or dismissed. There is power in people from the:

> Caribbean, East Africa, the Asian subcontinent, Pakistan, Bangladesh, from different parts of India, [who] all identified themselves politically as Black. What they said was, 'We may be different [in terms of] actual color skins but vis-a-vis the social system, vis-a-vis the political system of racism, there is more that unites us than what divides us.'
>
> (Hall, 1991: 55)

This alliance has been a source of strength in educational and wider movements against racism. As we saw in Chapter 1, the Black Parents Movement (BPM, nd: 1) defined its mission as being: 'To defend the interests of the black population of Caribbean, African, and Asian origin, especially the working class and unemployed section, and the general interests of the working class in Britain as a whole.'

However, political blackness was not consistently applied to the movement. Although the BPM embraced a somewhat politically black position, their founding document opened by admitting that the group was predominantly African and Caribbean and made a specific connection to the African American struggle.

The campaigns for equality in schooling contributed to wider movements for social justice that included more than the Black population. However, the use of political blackness as a vehicle for unity of minority groups is a misstep for a number of reasons. Primary among these is that it fails to capture the political nature of the Blackness that is defined in African ancestry. The declaration of Blackness is intrinsically bound up with the reclamation of pride in the African Diaspora. Political blackness delegitimizes this connection by attempting a much broader definition.

All of the participants in my study constructed Black groups as separate from other minorities. Jason was even wary about using the term 'Black' because he did not want to be mistaken as having a politically black point of view:

> I'll say African Caribbean as opposed to Black because we do have, in England, some people do say Asian people are Black. Some don't recognize that, so I make the distinction.

When I asked Errol to define Blackness he was quick to distance himself from the political black position that is embodied in the term 'Black and Minority Ethnic' (BME):

> Well we define Black specifically, so we don't do this whole BME thing that gets [things] messed up. We don't do all of that you

know. Black is African Caribbean as far as we're concerned and dual heritage.

The only participant who included other minorities in her definition of Blackness was Gloria. After explaining how African, Caribbean, and mixed heritage people were Black she added that Asians were too, though she said that 'Some accept the fact, or embrace the fact that they are Black. Even though they're Asian, they say that they're Black. Others won't.'

When I asked her a further question about whether Asians are considered Black she replied, 'Would I say Indians are Black? ... The only way I could answer that is that they're Black in an Indian sense of Black. They're not African Black.'

It is clear that Gloria is not wholly subscribing to a politically black definition. On the one hand she says Asians are Black but on the other she explains that they are not 'African Black'. Throughout her interview she constructed the Asian community as being separate from the Black community. Modood (1994) argued that political blackness reifies the Black/White dualism and marginalizes diverse Asian voices under the blanket of non-White homogeneity. The term 'BME', common in race relations parlance, speaks volumes about how this dualism is still being reinforced.

Just because some people in the Black supplementary school movement reject the concept of political blackness does not make it regressive. Neither does the fact that the state has abused the idea in its use of 'BME'. What critically undermines the idea of political blackness is that it does not recognize that claiming Blackness is itself a political statement. Furthermore, defining Blackness in relation to racism disempowers ethnic minority groups.

Political blackness draws disparate groups of people together, defining them in relation to the White British subject that they are not. As such the concept is characterized by *non-Whiteism*. Whiteness is placed in a normatively dominant position and naturalized by this view. Blackness becomes defined entirely in relation to Whiteness and all the power in this equation is with the dominant, the normal, the White. In terms of theory and practice this is one of the most damaging things minority groups can do because it confines the struggle for freedom within a framework created by the dominant. Stokely Carmichael argued that 'the first need of a free people is to define their own terms' (Tucker, 2004: 79) and non-Whiteism therefore presents serious limitations to emancipatory theory and practice.

The limits of the framework of political blackness are demonstrated in its most serious theoretical mistake: a national analysis of race and racism. While it is pragmatic for minority communities in a country to work together, racism is a global not a national system. National attitudes and policy are a manifestation of a global system of racism that has developed over four centuries. Political blackness relies on an insular national view to fight racism, which leads to irrational conclusions in theory and practice.

In the UK, a good example of this is the fight against inequality in education. From the perspective of political blackness, non-Whites should unite to fight racial discrimination in the system. However, examination of the statistics reveals that Indian and Chinese students outperform Whites. Pakistani, Bangladeshi, African, and African Caribbean children, however, achieve significantly lower grades (see Table 1 in Appendix). In addition, African Caribbean students have consistently been overrepresented in school exclusions (Parsons, 2009). There is no discrimination based on non-Whiteness in British schools and therefore political blackness does not provide a firm foundation for resistance.

At the global level, the homogenizing tendencies of political blackness unify the majority of the globe on the ontological experience of not being White. Even if we ignore the vast cultural differences, the idea that Western imperialism works on the matrix that those who are White exploit those who are not is too simplistic. There are disproportionate power relations across the globe between people who are not White. For example, China was indifferent towards apartheid South Africa (Kelley and Esch, 1999) and is now playing an increasingly neo-colonial role in the rest of the continent (Sprance, 2008). There are common goals for many non-Western countries, and some have united in ventures such as the Afro-Asian Bandung conference in 1955 (Wright, 2008). However, it is counterproductive to secure this unity on the basis of not being White.

Blackness, rooted in African ancestry, connects Black populations into a global Diaspora calling for the redemption of Africa. In doing so it is essential to fight colonialism and it is in this battle that unity with other ethnic groups and nations should be based. In the supplementary school movement this construction of Blackness was shown in calls for an African-centred education. Lorraine explained that embracing Africaness is not only about helping the Black community, but also 'about redefining who we are and how we want to be in this globalized world. When you redefine the African everything else has to change. It's about redefinition of relationship and identity and how we interact with each other on this planet.'

Anti-essentialist Blackness

The mis-theory of political blackness has led contemporary theorists to criticize the category of Black as too rigid and inflexible. Hall (1993) argues against closed identifications and explains the need for open, fluid identities that can incorporate difference and hybridity. Race, and therefore Blackness, is not seen as flexible enough to explain the fluidity of the so-called 'new' ethnicities. This necessitates disentangling the Black/White dualism that is said to restrict the cultural expression of minority groups (St Louis, 2002). However, the taboo Black/White dualism is something drawn from the definition of political blackness.

Political blackness is based on the premise that not being White predisposes people to embrace each other and their battles. Political blackness relies on a diverse range of people and communities, with their own issues and interests, to take up the causes of all who are not White. There are tensions between minority communities in the UK – for example, the 2005 riots between Caribbean and Muslim youth in Birmingham (John, 2005). Rather than understanding these tensions as being between different groups with competing interests, I have witnessed politically black campaigners lambasting the communities for not comprehending that they are all in the struggle together. Political blackness reifies the Black/White dualism, creating an inflexible category of 'blackness'.

Blackness rooted in African ancestry does not exist in the rigid form attributed to it by authors such as Gilroy (2002). Lemelle (1993) criticizes the idea of Afrocentricity because it reduces diverse cultural perspectives of Black populations to a homogeneous outlook. Such authors are fearful of the reductive forms of Blackness to which Nazroo and Karlsen (2003) found some younger Black Caribbeans subscribed. Unlike other minority groups, they were more likely than their older counterparts to hold 'traditional' views: being against interracial marriage, feeling more Black than British, and finding that it was more important to dress Black in public. The fear of restrictive forms of Blackness is valid but it is necessary to distinguish between cultural and political essentialism. In a cultural essentialism the ways in which a Black person should dress, talk, and act are restricted. This has been criticized as culturally nationalist and rejected by more progressive forms of Blackness (Carmichael, 1971).

Often overlooked when discussing Blackness in its political sense is the fact that although Black is used to encompass a varied group of people, it is not assumed that everyone under the umbrella should act or be the same. People are simply said to be connected by their African ancestry to form a global Diaspora. This ancestry plays a central role in framing the cultures and experiences of Black people across the globe, contrary to the claims of Marxist authors such as Harris, who claims that 'the life of the Negro in the United States bespeaks knowledge only of those cultural traditions which are

American ... nor can the American Negro be considered in any logical sense African' (1927: 469).

Although the cultures of the Diaspora are framed by African ancestry and history, they take on differing forms in their given contexts. A good example is the development of Hip Hop in America and the emergence of Grime music in Britain. Both are based on the heavy bass and drumbeats from the African continent, and the lyrical style of rap in each genre is descended from a Jamaican reggae form of toasting. Although they are very different musical styles, with their own parochial influences, they are classed as Black music because of their roots in African culture.

Under the umbrella of Blackness there are myriad identities. All have their own meanings and definitions. This diversity in Blackness led William Cross to alter his foundational Black Racial Identity model. Although he kept the notion of people progressing through stages until they reached a positive Black identity, Cross (1991) added a range of identity positions to capture the diversity of African American identity. Black Racial Identity research has since evolved and Sellers *et al.* (1998) capture the mood of the discipline with their 'Multidimensional Inventory of Black Identity' (MIBI). In this model, Blackness is seen as one part of a person's identity, which will have varying import to different people. Four ideological positions are identified to which a person may subscribe in relation to their Blackness: assimilationist, nationalist, multiculuralist, and humanist. These are not seen as either/or ideologies: a person may subscribe to all of them, but to differing degrees. Blackness is seen as flexible, depending on the situation.

My participants constructed a fluid and connective Blackness. When Clive discussed the different motivations of parents to take their children to supplementary schools he said, 'it's the community isn't it, so you get a range of responses'. He did not view the Black community as homogeneous but as one that would produce a diverse set of reactions.

The Black community was also constructed as having no physical boundaries in the interviews. Black supplementary schools were not being run on a localized basis, as Rose and Henry described:

> KA: Do most of the students come from the area, from quite close?
> Rose: Not, not close, five miles, further, round the city. I've got children from different areas.
> Henry: Because I remember in the early times, when I used to have the van, I used to pick up maybe about half a dozen, eight children from around the city.

Many of the supplementary schools in my study drew students from large areas of their respective cities. In one of the cities where the research took place, Henry described the changing nature of the Black community:

> If you look at the Black population [of the city] – when I say Black population I'm talking about African Caribbean or African population – we are not concentrated in one particular way ... We used to be. I've found that we are more patchy, spread out more than concentrated in one place.

Although the location of the community has changed, the networks have remained open. For instance, 'word of mouth' was the most common method of attracting students to supplementary schools. The diverse, delocalized community is essential to understanding a fluid and open Blackness. Gloria described different communities within the larger Black one, like the 'old', the 'young', and the 'upcoming middle class'. She said these communities had different priorities and ideas, but they all linked together because of their 'culture and histories'.

Blackness as a collective

With its anti-foundationalism and anti-essentialist propositions, postmodern identity theory reduces Blackness to the 'difference that makes no difference' (Hall, 1993: 361). A postmodern, fractured, fluid, and de-essentialized world heralds the end of race as an explanatory or emancipatory category (Gilroy, 1998). In Britain, race has been largely replaced with ethnicity and cultural difference (Alexander and Alleyne, 2002). These are seen to exist because they are based on commonalities of culture, heritage, language, and custom (Jenkins, 2005). Modood (1996) argues that our attempts should be focused on freeing these real ethnic collectives from the yoke of discrimination. Race is not seen as a basis upon which to found a real collective.

The 'ethnicity instead of race' approach delegitimizes Blackness as the basis of a real collective. Faced with such diversity and the wealth of so-called new ethnicities, St Louis (2002) presents the quandary of uniting this multitude of ethnicities into a cohesive political movement. For instance, the 'strong Black woman' and the 'young Black man' will have divergent experiences and therefore construct their Blackness differently. However, what the postmodern argument misses is that Blackness does not depend on absolute agreement at micro level. Though the strong Black woman and the young Black man may construct different daily meanings of their being Black, it is their commitment to Blackness at the macro level that is essential.

Conclusion

The danger in the theoretical misconceptions of race is that they delegitimize the union of Blackness, which is necessary for Black people to fight inequality. Collective action based on a shared identity remains an avenue to seriously challenge inequities within the social system. Supplementary schools are an example of how Black communities have rallied and organized around the idea of Blackness. Blackness rooted in African ancestry is the glue that holds the Black supplementary school movement together. But the movement is not a completely unified collective and there are different, and somewhat competing, ideologies that define Black supplementary schools. Blackness is articulated differently across the movement and the next chapter examines the underlying tensions and principles of Black supplementary education.

Chapter 3
The organization and philosophies of supplementary schools

The Black supplementary schooling movement is marked by a diversity of approaches and philosophies. This chapter explores the differences in the ways that funding and curriculum operate in the programmes and, essentially, the place of politics within them. A broad distinction exists between the 'official' and the 'self-help' projects, determined by their level of professionalism and their relationship with the state. Though there are significant ideological and practical differences, Black supplementary schools all share the principle that a Black-led environment is an essential element of the education of Black children.

Grassroots organization

Black supplementary schools arose in response to the vicious racial inequalities that have faced the African Caribbean community since their arrival in Britain (Carby, 1983; Chevannes and Reeves, 1989). Clive attested to the development of supplementary schools when responding to a question on why they started their project:

> Historically it's because Black people have been disadvantaged, it's like a community response to the fact that our children have been, at first it was just miseducated, but bottom line it's abused, neglected.

Grosvenor (1997: 152) explains how this runs contrary to the popular discourse of the Black community in which they are often depicted as passive victims being acted upon by others:

> The history of the black presence in Britain is characterized not by political inaction but by concerted action against injustice, not by accommodation but by organized resistance to racism in education.

Growing as it did out of community concern for the education of the young, the supplementary school movement was initially run as a voluntary endeavour (Best, 1990; Chevannes and Reeves, 1989). Volunteers would organize extra tuition when they had time outside of work hours and usually on Saturdays, which is why they are often referred to as Saturday schools. However, they are not run exclusively at the weekends. Rose organized her supplementary school on a Sunday and Angela explains why their supplementary school ran in the evenings:

> We were purely voluntary, we needed our jobs to get our money, so it was only when we had some time available, which was the evenings.

As well as schools that run alongside the school year, summer schools are organized for the holidays. Thus a Black supplementary school is any organization that arranges extra education for the Black community outside mainstream school provision. Supplementary schools are common among other minority groups, but the Black supplementary school is unique in that it is not based on teaching religion or language (Hall *et al.*, 2002; Martin *et al.*, 2003).

Black supplementary schools are grassroots organizations started by people in the community who want to make a difference. Angela told the story of how she and her partner set up their evening school:

> We had contacts with a number of Black parents who were extremely anxious about what was gonna happen to their children. So because of that reason we thought we [would] try and do something ... we had some skills and we felt we could help some young people to succeed ... We didn't know exactly how to do it ... we were involved in a Black church, with a Black pastor very close to here, said okay well 'how are we gonna do it?' None of us had big houses to actually start the night school, and in fact we actually approach the minister, he agreed and allow us to use the church, in the night, to teach the children.

The grassroots foundation of the movement led to a range of supplementary schools being developed. Essentially, the schools emerged in the location and form that the people running them could organize. As Kwame described:

> You had individuals who were academic who decided they wanted to progress their children's education. So you also had organizations who were there set up to try and aid equality for

The organization and philosophies of supplementary schools

want of a better word ... So you had people educating children within their homes, just to accelerate the process and give them an even playing field so to speak, so again Saturday schools then mushroom from the many Black organizations around the country, Manchester, London, and so forth.

The way the movement has developed, on a small scale in local communities, has meant there has been little overall coordination. Various organizations have developed and then receded, such as the National Association of Black Supplementary Schools, which was active in London during the 1980s, hosting conferences and attempting to bring different schools together. In 2007, a new National Association of Black Supplementary Schools (NABSS) was launched, the aim of which is to deal with the 'lack of cohesion and also a lack of information readily available' between different projects. It was set up to 'be a central resource for parents, members, and helpers of the Afrikan/Caribbean descent community to find help with their children's education in their locality' (NABSS, 2011: np).

NABSS was constituted to fill the need of connecting the disparate supplementary school groups. Their website provides resources that can be used for teaching, as well as links to potential workshop coordinators for lessons. They also highlight a key problem facing the development of the Black supplementary school movement: being run on a voluntary basis means there is little money for advertisement so parents are often unaware of supplementary schools in their community. NABSS encapsulates this concern by having a clearly stated objective, to 'make sure the excuse of "I can't find a supplementary school" is no longer valid' (NABSS, 2011: np). To combat this, the website carries a directory of supplementary school programmes set up in cities around the country. The story of how this directory began is indicative of the grassroots and fragmented nature of the movement. Nia, who runs the organization, told me:

> I was at a film event, where the organizers had invited all the Black Saturday schools that they knew. When we got there, there were seven Black Saturday schools and I thought this is great, all these Black Saturday schools we should network with each other, and communicate. So before the film started me and my bold self I stepped up to the front and said, 'listen, we have a few Black Saturday schools in here, so at the end of the film if someone from each Saturday school could come to the front then we can exchange each others' details and keep in touch'... At the end of the film, I waited at the bottom of the stairs and no one turned up.

> I thought no man, this is out of order, how can we have all these Black Saturday schools with the same agenda in the same room and we're not communicating?

In response, Nia set about building a directory of supplementary schools by gathering the information through word of mouth. The directory currently carries information on over 60 supplementary schools across the country. Given the lack of communication between projects this is quite an achievement, and much of the research for this book would not have been possible without Nia's endeavours.

The grassroots nature of the movement makes it impossible to track student numbers over the years because there are no records of so many of the supplementary school programmes that existed. Programmes have emerged and then closed without any contact with the wider movement. Plus, the supplementary schools that are known about do not necessarily keep longstanding records of attendance. So there can never be a reliable picture of the number of programmes, their different types, or the number of children who have attended. Consequently, this book can set out only the general trends in the movement and the underpinning philosophies of the different types of organization in Black supplementary schools.

Typically, Black supplementary schools are small, with a small number of students, to enable volunteers to cope with the work (Issa and Williams, 2009). However, the number of students in the supplementary schools researched for this book ranged from 10 to over 100. Many of the participants in the current study spoke of the need to keep the numbers down to, as Jason put it, keep the project 'manageable'.

The students accepted by the supplementary schools in this study ranged in age from 4 to 16. All projects targeted the full statutory age range, except for Kwame's, which focused on 5 to 12 year olds, and Errol's, which taught 9 to 15 year olds. The schools aim to promote education and learning for youths in the community, so an open age range is important. Typically attendance drops as children grow older. This was largely put down to the difficulty in persuading older children to attend, but there was also concern about the expertise required to teach older students. Clive expressed the problem:

> We ran from 4 up to 14/15, our limiting factor was on the top end having the expertise to deliver GCSE stuff, okay, so if we lost that then we couldn't deliver.

The organization and philosophies of supplementary schools

Such concerns over expertise and delivering for examinations highlight the key development in the supplementary school: the move away from concerned volunteer organizations towards being more professionalized and having trained teachers and 'experts' on board. Clive charted this development in relation to a different school in another part of the city:

> I think when Saturday schools first started we were not as organized as we are now. You've got a high level of education in the community, so you can have schools like the ones which are staffed fully by teachers, an incredible scenario. They're able to draw down funding. My experience has always been largely voluntary, and so we get some qualified staff, some concerned parents, some concerned individuals come together, to try to deal with, the perceived problems of miseducation in the short term and in the wider community long term.

The move towards professionalism is related to the changing relationship between Black supplementary schools and the state, particularly with regard to funding.

State funding

All of the functioning supplementary schools in the study bar Kwame's had received some state funding for at least part of their existence. This is an interesting development, since relations between Black supplementary schools and the local councils have been fractious at times (Best, 1990). Originally, local councils and schools could be sceptical of what they thought were uneducated Black people taking teaching into their own hands (Tomlinson, 1988). However, if the quality of educational provision delivered to Black young people was of genuine concern, the state would not have consigned them to secondary modern and special education schools. In reality, the local councils feared Black radicalism would be taught in the supplementary schools.

Menelik was involved in one of the earliest supplementary schools and saw the relationship to the state as a battle. He spoke about a meeting where the head of the LEA told those organizing the supplementary school that if it were up to him he would 'lock them up and throw away the key...', adding:

> So after that we was going for a while and settling down and the propaganda about these trained Black extremists, race haters, and future terrorists and all this rubbish, kinda just dies out. But that wasn't all of it because the government itself had an idea about

the Saturday school and it wanted to smash it. So they started this thing about telling parents that we're extremists and then it [would] never work. So what they did was they start[ed to] run to the parents to find out who the children are who go to the Saturday school, and aksing [sic] them to put up their hand in the schools. Teachers say 'do you go to the Saturday school?' and then [once] they put up their hand they would be ignored and they'd be victimized. So these are some of the things, this is the history of this Saturday school movement.

The accommodation of supplementary schools by the local authority today is very different. Supplementary education now appears to be part of the government's agenda on education, as Kwame extolled:

> The schools [mainstream] are now open on Saturdays. We've looked at Walsall, we've looked at Wolverhampton, we've looked at Birmingham, most of those schools open on Saturdays are now attended by the Asians so they're now doing supplementary school of some form.

Things have changed dramatically from the days of the pitched battles with the state described by Menelik. In Clive's words:

> If you look at, look, the seventies was when we kicked off and we've come a long way, to a degree we're part of the state now, they see us, they recognize us and they fund us.

However, the attack by the state, even in the early period, was never total. A hallmark of the Black supplementary school movement is its diversity. Most of the schools in this research had little contact with other programmes. Just as there are varied understandings of Blackness, Black supplementary schools are also diverse. While Menelik and his group were being hounded by the police and the LEA for suspected Black radicalism, Angela was organizing a project that had the support of the LEA and was housed in a school building.

In the 1970s local councils were also involved in the delivery and funding of supplementary school projects. As outlined in Chapter 1, the George Padmore and Albertina Sylvester schools sought funding from the LEA to expand their provision and received a state grant from the Institute of Race Relations. Menelik's experience of the state was not true of all supplementary schools.

In 1987 the Inner London Education Authority (ILEA) hosted a conference on supplementary schooling with funding from the Department

The organization and philosophies of supplementary schools

of Education and Science, the Home Office, and the Department of the Environment. This does not indicate a picture of supplementary schools as outside the remit of state funding and influence. In fact, state funds were essential to the organization of certain Black supplementary schools. As we have seen, Black supplementary schools are 'a direct result of the failure of the British Education System to educate our [African Caribbean] children adequately' (Association of Supplementary Schools, nd: 1). At the same conference, Valentino Jones asserted that it is 'too much to ask our communities to pay twice for their children's education on top of all the other support they give. We look to the ILEA for funding as a right and not as a privilege' (Jones, 1987: 4). As Black supplementary schools are conceived of as doing a job of which the mainstream schools are incapable, the state should therefore be contributing funds.

While they did not share the overt critique of the mainstream school system, the ILEA agreed that the Black supplementary school movement had an important role. Not only did they host the conference but the deputy head of the ILEA, Bernard Wiltshire, declared his hopes that 'supplementary school will have a permanent structured place in London's educational system' (Wiltshire, 1987: 5). This support is explored in Chapter 4: I point out here that the state was keen to fund certain Black supplementary school projects, who in turn expected support from the authorities.

The diametrically opposed experiences of Menelik and Angela in their dealings with the education authorities was due partly to their being in different LEAs. More importantly, Menelik's supplementary school was part of a wider radical political organization with ties to groups such as the Black Panthers. Neither the state nor society has been keen to understand, let alone embrace, the politics of Black Power. In Carby's words, 'just as the sociology of race relations was to ignore the implications of increasingly militant black political consciousness, so educational theory advocated avoidance, at all costs, of black power politics' (Carby, 1983: 193).

Thus the Black supplementary school projects are clearly underpinned by the different philosophies and politics behind them.

Official vs. self-help

In her study of Black supplementary schools, Stone (1981) drew a distinction between 'official' and 'self-help' projects. Official projects are funded by the state and are more likely to pay qualified teachers and monitor standards. Self-help projects are voluntary, lie outside the state educational policy, and, according to Stone, are 'responsible to no one, supervised by no one, and accountable to no one' (1981: 177). This distinction between official and self-help is the fault line in the Black supplementary school movement. In her study on supplementary schools, Dove found that there were on the one hand schools like 'School A [which] sees its role as liberating children from psychological, emotional, moral, and spiritual oppression in a struggle for Black equality' and on the other, schools like 'School C [which] sees its role as tutoring, confidence building, and encouraging excellence' (Dove, 1991: 91).

Drawing a distinction between official and self-help projects helps to clarify the difference in relationships between the supplementary schools and the state. The autonomy of the self-help projects has no doubt been a source of anxiety for various state institutions in the past, and was the reason they wished to bring the sector under the remit of the local councils.

The relationship between the state and Black supplementary schools is not simply about governmental attitudes and politics. Even official Black supplementary schools have been wary of government involvement lest they find themselves co-opted (Best, 1990). One of the central debates for Black supplementary schools has been over 'the acceptance of government funds', in the 'desire to maintain autonomy from the state' (Dove, 1993: 444). For the coalition of state and supplementary schools to continue there must be a certain amount of faith in the government to provide for the Black community.

Jason ran one of the most professionalized of the supplementary schools in the study, employing qualified teachers and monitoring its performance and effectiveness. The project had started out as a voluntary organization, but the search for funding compelled them to produce evidence of the positive outcomes of the school. He explained the value of receiving funding:

> That's the difference that funding makes, because you have to justify your outcome, so it's being able to do that. Tracking that got us additional years' funding because we were able to say look, 'X, Y, and Z are attending this school and attained higher than Sandwell's average'. Now if you, if you translate that, if African Caribbean children, boys and girls, are below Sandwell's average, and we've got students who are actually attaining above Sandwell's average, the gap is quite wide, so yes it does work. Particularly, and if you're geared up to academic attainment, as a Saturday school, if you can get your tracking system right, you can show that it works.

Helping children succeed by being geared to what he calls 'academic attainment' is buttressed by the funding but also by the effort to secure those funds. Other participants spoke in similar terms: funding from the state led to better resources and also the need to meet what Clive called particular 'standards'.

The drive to regulate standards in the supplementary school is embodied in the increasing presence of accreditation schemes. This includes the Quality Framework run by an educational charity called ContinYou, which was most widely referenced during the interviews. ContinYou (2011: np) explains the Quality Framework as a 'voluntary quality recognition scheme, which is independent, peer-assessed, and self-regulated. It is run for and by supplementary schools and those who support them. It aims to celebrate and record the achievements of supplementary schools and improve quality across the sector.'

The framework has three levels of award: Gold, Silver, and Bronze. Supplementary schools have to demonstrate effective leadership and management alongside innovative approaches to teaching and learning.

Pascale Vassie, who works for the organization, said the importance of attaining recognition awards was that supplementary schools could 'prove that they're making a difference'. She maintained that the original driver behind the formation of the resource unit for supplementary schools and accreditation was the funders (education authorities and charities). These funders received a number of applications for money from various supplementary schools and they thought there needed to be greater coordination between the programmes. According to Pascale:

> Some local authorities have tied achievement of the award to the local authority funding, so they've said that you have to have the Bronze. It's not that they weren't asking for those things [in the award] anyway, but linking their funding to the Bronze award [makes it] easier. Haringey, Lewisham, Leicester, Milton Keynes, they've said if we're going to provide you with funding you need to have the Bronze Quality Framework. Some local authorities, for instance, Leicester, they have said we will pay you each time you achieve another level of the framework. I think it might be £500 just to help you get the Gold.

Supplementary school accreditation thus relates to the increasing presence of the state in the movement. The Quality Framework encourages supplementary schools to form partnerships with mainstream schools so that, as Pascale explained, they 'can see what difference it's making to the key stage assessments'. At the higher levels of the framework, baseline and term-by-term assessments of the students' progress is expected. To achieve the Gold award she said that they were 'looking for regular CPD and training for teachers throughout the year. We'd be looking for them to have a teaching qualification, either at home or here, but to have a clear idea of how children learn and how to support them.'

Pascale was keen to stress that there were no restrictions as to what could be taught in the supplementary schools and no proscriptions as to forms of assessments. She cited as an example a programme that was focused on Black history and used debates as a form of assessment. However, it is clear from the expectations of qualified teachers, assessment, and partnerships with schools, especially in the higher levels, that an effort is being made to bring the standards of mainstream schooling into supplementary education. Most of the projects ContinYou work with are focused on bilingualism and mother-tongue maintenance, so are not Black supplementary schools. For such programmes, accommodation into mainstream schooling has not been such a complicated issue because they are not explicitly based on an indictment of the school system. Palsent, whose programme had achieved the Bronze award, sounded some caution about the assessment process:

> It's good in a certain way but you've got to put in resources to do that ... A lot of the extra things that they sometimes ask you to do, it's quite time consuming and it can take away from our focus. Just like at school when teachers say that when Ofsted comes in everyone is concentrating on getting the paperwork right. The children are just kind of in the background almost, preparing for a certain kind of exam and the real education isn't going on. So we have to be careful that we don't fall into that same kind of trap where you end up putting your energies into getting some kind of an award.

The dangers of becoming too much like the mainstream schools are also highlighted by Sonia, who has noted the change in emphasis over the past 20 years. The focus is now on attainment and the mainstream curriculum, which Sonia feels is:

> A shame because then you become more or less like an ordinary school and I suppose [you have to ask] whether or not you really want that because I think that what was unique about the Saturday schools was that they did their own thing, away from the school, but I guess there was more and more sort of pressure to mimic the school.

Jason sounds a fundamental alarm about the trend of professionalization. He believes the increased funding and focus on outcomes changed the very nature of Black supplementary schools:

> At first it was very much volunteers who weren't trained as teachers so they were very much, much more focused on African history, Caribbean history, sort of raising self-esteem in that way. It's moved now that the African history has taken not so much a back seat but it has a lower profile, what's taken the profile now is academic attainment.

So while originally the focus in his project was on cultural education, academic outcomes have now taken precedence. Whether to focus on academic attainment or cultural learning has been a key dilemma throughout the history of the Black supplementary school movement.

Academic vs. cultural learning

Teaching Black youth the fundamental skills of learning is a major motivation of Black supplementary schools (Reeves and Chevannes, 1983b). Stone (1981: 97) argues that 'acquiring basic educational skills was the basis of what went on in supplementary schools'. At the same time, it was from the outset an aim to provide some cultural learning that is missing in the mainstream schools system. The Caribbean Education and Community Workers Association express this in their statement:

> The aim of these [supplementary schools] is to provide opportunity for guidance and for discussion of Black history and culture while at the same time giving assistance in the normal school subjects in order to encourage Black children to make the most of their stay in Primary and Secondary schools.
>
> (CECWA, 1971: 2)

At times, however, the two principles have been in conflict within the movement because it can be difficult to strike a balance between them (Reay and Mirza, 1997; Stone, 1981). More often an either/or approach has been adopted and typically the two goals are viewed as separate. For example, in the George Padmore and Albertina Sylvester schools there were different sessions for academic subjects and Black history, culture, and politics. This raises the question of priorities, as the time to work with students is so limited in supplementary schools.

The importance of Black history and culture was often mentioned by participants in my research, but the goal of academic attainment was generally paramount. Inequality has increasingly become defined in terms of 'differences in outcome' (Steven, 2007: 170) and most of the participants thought this way. Attainment at GCSE level was the goal of most projects, which sought access to university and the better job prospects that such achievement brings. Menelik, however, had an entirely different construction of success and achievement in Black supplementary schooling. He was the only participant not to mention school grades and to give priority instead to the role of Black cultural and historical learning. An understanding of themselves and others as Black people, and an historical appreciation of the meaning of this, seemed to be the aim for his project. That is not to say that he did not value university attendance and employment, but what was key was educating the youth about issues that affect them as Black people. It is here that Black supplementary schools can offer something different from mainstream schooling.

Criticism has been levelled at the emphasis on Black culture and history because, as Jason observed, 'there's no point in learning Black culture if you can't read or write'. Teaching the core skills on one hand and Black culture and history on the other are not competing issues for Menelik. Basic educational skills were still a priority but they were addressed through Black studies, which is not uncommon in the movement (Reeves and Chevannes, 1983b). For example, in the George Padmore and Albertina Sylvester schools much of the work that went on was reading comprehension, which was meant to aid in the study of English at school. However, the texts they selected for these exercises were Black literature, including some very radical works (see Chapter 1). In one exercise the students read an extract from the classic book by George Jackson, a Black Panther who was killed during a prison riot, *Soledad Brother*. After students had read the extract, they were asked the following questions for reading comprehension:

1. Jackson wonders why so many white men have had the wish to rule over other people's countries and control their lives. Why do you think they have done this?

2. Give some examples of countries that English people have ruled over.

3. How important is it to have flashy clothes and plenty of money?

4. Why does Jackson have no time for people who think flashy clothes and money are important?

5. Why were prisoners forced to march everywhere?

(Comprehension, nd)

The organization and philosophies of supplementary schools

It is clear how an exercise designed to assist the students' mainstream performance is also intrinsic to teaching Black history and culture. So the teaching of Black studies is not necessarily at odds with reinforcing the 3Rs. The majority of the participants spoke about using similar methods to teach Black history and culture. Crucially, though, these methods were often constructed as precisely that: to teach the Black studies element. Black studies remained separate from mainstream academic subjects and an effort was put into making Black studies useful to the students in their mainstream schools. Every programme analysed in this research involved the use of mainstream curricular worksheets and materials, even in the most radical self-help programme, as I discuss in Chapter 7.

The use of school worksheets further illustrates the core of the movement: mainstream success. Teaching methods frequently overlap with mainstream school, especially in the case of official projects, which often enlist trained teachers. Such an extension of mainstream schooling has obvious benefits in preparing students for exams and school work. However, there has been dissent from those inside the movement at approaches that follow mainstream schooling too closely. Jocelyn Barrow argued at a West Indian Educationists (WIE, nd) meeting in the early period of the movement:

> I think also it is sad from the child's point of view to have a continuation of school to home. What we can do is put in what I call, for want of a better word, an enrichment programme for the child, where you are exposing him to a series of things, you are stimulating his curiosity, you are getting him interested in things, looking to see how things work and so on, and that sort of enrichment helps him to get on with school work rather than plodding away at the school material again, because to my mind you are making [supplementary] school a very distasteful place.

Barrow is arguing for a different conception of the teaching that should take place in Black supplementary schools. It is clear that she wants the work of the programmes to support mainstream schooling but wants this done by engaging students on levels that interest them and are distinct from mainstream school practice. However, Barrow notes that her position was a 'personal view added to a minority opinion given by the Working Party' of the WIE (*ibid.*: 7). The same can be said for the situation in the Black supplementary school movement as a whole, where for the most part the methods and resources from mainstream schools are embraced, particularly in the teaching of the mainstream school subjects.

Pedagogically, Black supplementary schools generally do not offer a radical critique of the methods of instruction used in mainstream schooling. There is no Freirean (1972) call for revolutionizing the teacher–student relationship or democratizing knowledge. The critique of schooling presented by Black supplementary schools is primarily that Black children are not treated fairly in the mainstream and that the curriculum fails to reflect their history and culture, thus placing them at further disadvantage. Certainly official supplementary schools are seen to be extending the work of the mainstream school system. This is why the state has been able to embrace segments of the movement.

Political education

The question of politics and how much of a role it should play in education also arises. Once again, Menelik had very different ideas from the other interviewees, and his supplementary school was the most radical of those examined for this research in the sense of being connected to a Pan-African organization. Politics was essential to both the founding of his project and its curriculum. His supplementary school had links to American groups such as the Sundiata Liberation Center for Children (1969: 1), who saw their role as to develop:

> African Revolutionaries ... to do more than raise the consciousness of Black children but to activate the Pan-Africanist concepts and develop them ... [and] provide practical and viable skills for mental, physical, and mainly political development and maintenance of our children.

As we saw, the New Beacon supplementary schools also directly politicized education in their programmes in their choice of readings and exercises, presenting students with the politics of Black liberation. Even the study of traditional subjects was politicized. One young man who attended the school wrote that when he grows up he wants to do 'something which will enable me to be useful to Black people in Africa and the Americas. In this respect maths and science will be important to concentrate on' (Homework, nd: 1).

Politics in the supplementary school movement is not always quite as radical or tied into global issues of Black liberation. From the beginning, however, supplementary schools strove to influence how the politics of schooling works in Britain. In the Black Parents Movement's document of 1981, dealing with training for those working in supplementary schools, Black consciousness and history are included under the heading 'politicization of supplementary school workers'. This, though, is ranked beneath the two goals of being aware of the 'politics of the LEAS and how to cope both politically and administratively', and the role of 'mediating between parents, children, and schools' (BPM, 1981: 2). The goal of trying to influence mainstream schooling and help the parents and children to navigate the schools has been a major focus of the supplementary school movement. The Association of Supplementary Schools called for:

> Active involvement in the development of a new mainstream education curriculum. ILEA should approach the proposed Association of Supplementary Schools for guidance and assistance in their policy making.
> (Association of Supplementary Schools, 1987: 9)

Politics played a major role throughout. However, there were participants in the study who focused on criticizing the school system for failing the Black community yet did not make the supplementary schools themselves the arena for political battles. Angela, in particular, was clear about a non-political position for her supplementary project, when it was running:

> We did not see the school as an arena for a political battle to be fought about those Black children. While some of the Black supplementary school, they actually use those as political battlegrounds, what we did because we're all members of political parties, we took those issues in to the political parties and didn't implicate or misuse those children. We felt they were already being misused through an education system that was letting them down and so we should not be working out our own, if you like unease and discontentment, on them. We use that in our own political processes to get change.

Official projects can show reluctance to engage in the political arena within the schools. A one-day conference of the National Association of Black Supplementary Schools (NABSS) in 1982 included a workshop entitled 'Should Black supplementary schools, as part of their curriculum, deal with social and political issues?' (NABSS, 1982: 2). For official projects, political and social issues were not an inevitable aspect of the programmes. Another workshop session, entitled 'Are Black supplementary schools involved enough in the black struggle?', indicated the critique that was levied at the official projects at the time. So while some supplementary schools, such as those around New Beacon, were actively linked into wider political movements and discourse, others were connected to wider political struggles only by way of ensuring that Black students could succeed in mainstream schools.

As in all matters, an apolitical stance is still a political position, and staying above the fray has implications for official projects. Best (1990: 165) argues that 'no supplementary school worth its salt can afford not to be political' because the right to criticize and challenge the state and the educational system are seen as paramount. When reliant on funding from outside the organization, the money and the criteria attached will always dictate to the organization its objectives and limitations. Crucially, this can stifle dissent from supplementary schools because they have to 'avoid criticizing the funding agents' (*ibid.*: 165). Criticism of the local councils who fund them has, according to Errol, been the 'death knell' of many organizations. Importantly, a focus on attainment and slotting into the state sector of education amounts to a *de facto* commitment to and acceptance of mainstream ambitions and these can alter the nature of the programmes.

Jason felt that the demands that came with the money his school received from agencies meant that the study of Black history and culture was being lost. In order to satisfy the funders, the supplementary school had to provide evidence of success in mainstream school subjects, so the time they could devote to Black studies was curtailed. Jason believed that this lack of emphasis on the cultural side of the supplementary school has been detrimental. When asked where he thinks supplementary education will be in years to come he replied:

> I've got a feeling that they [will] move back towards a more cultural focus. They may do something where, it may be a cultural school which is more about culture and voluntary, so you know if you wanna child to learn about some issues around the civil rights movement stuff, within a sort of, different type of setting to the mainstream school, then it may be that.

Jason maintains that the cultural focus is tied up in the voluntary nature of supplementary schooling. He sees the Black studies element as separate from the goals the state has for supplementary education. Volunteerism to him means independence from funders and their concerns or wishes and therefore the freedom to teach the Black studies element that is neglected when supplementary schools have to work within the confines of funding applications. Errol, whose group did not rely on state funding to survive, describes some of the perils of relying on funding from the state:

> We like our independence, that gives us the ability to criticize if criticism is necessary and to say 'no we're not gonna do that because we don't think it works'. Whereas the government, and

I'm not blaming all parties, tend to dangle carrots and say 'if you jump this way then we'll give this, if you jump that way', and sometimes you have to say well, is that really what we want to do and we've found, that's been very frustrating for us where you want the funding but have to do something that's pretty much a waste of time for us.

To some extent this means that accepting money from the state equates to being subject to their politics. Alongside the lack of emphasis on Black history, culture, and certainly politics, Jason complains of the 'community cohesion agenda', which is moving away from targeted funding to specific groups. His supplementary school is being forced to open its doors to all groups in the area and not to specifically target Black students.

Community cohesion

Community cohesion is a recent development in British race relations, born out of the perceived crisis caused by the so-called 'death of multiculturalism' (Kundani, 2002: 67). Multiculturalism represented the British state's response to the abject failure of assimilationist policies for immigrants in the postwar period. In the 1960s the government realized that difference could not be ignored by clinging to an idyllic Britishness. An idea emerged of a nation made up of 'communities of communities' (Parekh, 2000: ix), where settling populations of migrants would be able to maintain ties with the cultures and traditions they brought with them. The state recognized differences of ethnicity and culture and provided funding to groups supporting communities of faith and culture.

However, since the Bradford and Oldham riots, and the terrorist attacks on the World Trade Center and London Underground, there has been a significant backlash against the multiculturalism model (Vertovec, 2002). The doctrine of recognizing and funding different cultural and ethnic groups is said to cause communities to develop separate lives and outlooks and therefore to breed mistrust between communities and towards the state (McGhee, 2005). Accordingly, New Labour brought in an era of community cohesion, where funding would no longer focus on supporting different groups but rather on activities that bring together communities of diverse backgrounds (Worley, 2005).

The community cohesion agenda has serious implications for the Black supplementary school movement. As highlighted in Chapter 2, what defines the movement is commitment to Blackness and therefore the spaces are predominantly Black-led and attended. Although Blackness has not been seen as a particularly legitimate form of organization by the state, supplementary schools have received state support due to their African Caribbean focus. Targeted funding to African Caribbean groups was a significant feature of the multiculturalism model (Afridi and Warmington, 2009). When Jason complains of what he sees as the 'community cohesion agenda' changing the nature of his project – as funding is increasingly removed from groups who target one community or ethnicity – it is in this context that he speaks. The removal of the Black studies element was also down to community cohesion in Jason's view, as he felt that this push to open up Black supplementary schools to other groups necessitated a more 'inclusive curriculum'. Herein lies the main flaw in the concept of community cohesion.

In theory, community cohesion aims to be inclusive, connecting citizens to a shared sense of Britishness while at the same time allowing for difference (Cantle, 2001). However, the policy is an astonishing step backwards in race relations, invoking the spirit of assimilation (Back *et al*., 2002). The idyllic Britishness to which citizens must subscribe is defined entirely on the presumed values of the White majority. It therefore 'others' the migrant communities who have been settled for decades (Kalra and Kapoor, 2009). It is based on the fear that the so-called separate lives that minorities (and in particular Muslims) are living creates not only civil unrest and distrust but also potential terrorists. Therefore it is minorities who can no longer be indulged with multiculturalism and who need to sign up to the community cohesion agenda.

In practice, although community cohesion does not legislate against difference, it makes efforts to discourage it, with the removal of funding and support for targeted groups. The Black supplementary school movement is one. There is pressure on the official projects to focus on mainstream attainment and to include a diverse range of children. Both requirements would mean a reduction in the teaching of Black studies. If Black supplementary schools lose the Black-led environment and no longer teach Black history, they will cease to be different from any after school or homework club. From the community cohesion perspective, opening up Black supplementary schools could appear to give White children an experience of a Black environment, but once opened up, the nature of the environment ceases to be Black-led and defined and becomes a normalized space of 'British' education. The state-directed community cohesion agenda threatens to alter fundamentally the very nature of the projects, so much so that Jason can envisage a time when the school is no longer Black and is simply an extra-tuition project.

Black environment

Jason was not alone in having his project forced to open up to other groups. Clive too is being compelled to open out the reach of the school to other communities. This change is fundamental: it is the predominantly Black environment that has always been key to the Black supplementary school movement. According to Reeves and Chevannes, 'the fraternity of colour is an important aspect of the schools' success in pupils' eyes' (1983b: 8). A Black environment is said to cut out some of the issues of race in the classroom dynamic, as Dove (1991: 106) explains:

> Supplementary schools provide the environment that supports the dignity and integrity of the Black child, unlike the circumstances in which the antagonist, dialectical nature of the Black/White teacher relations can manifest. This provides a basis for mutual respect.

It is this mutual respect that led participants in the research to describe the atmosphere in the Black supplementary schools as being more 'comfortable', and to children feeling more culturally included. For Sonia, the level of comfort in the supplementary school was translated into a different teacher–student relationship:

> I think it's a different relationship because there's a different vibe about the place. You come in, you know you have to do your piece of work, [that we] were not averse to telling you off and you can't run home and say you know this teacher (laughs). We're going to talk to you just how your mom or grandmom or auntie speaks to you and we're not taking any nonsense, not taking any excuses as [to] why you didn't do the piece of homework.

The Black-led space has also been seen as important as somewhere for Black children, parents, and volunteers outside of the mainstream system to be able to discuss and confront issues in education and society, and this space has been vital throughout the movement. Resistance to opening the doors to everyone must be seen in this context.

It is also the case that although a predominantly Black environment is central to the supplementary schools, virtually all of the participants were adamant that they would teach all children who came through the door. As Rose put it:

> I just see children as children, whether Black or White. If a White child is having problems in school I can teach that White child. Number one, where I'm from in Jamaica I went to school with

> English children because we had English people living in the area. So if the White parent is willing to send their child to this school we'll teach them.

Including other groups did not entail any major philosophical adjustments for most of the supplementary schools in the study. There was no objection to the inclusion of other groups on grounds of ill feeling towards them or of not promoting mixing with their children. The objections should be seen in the same way as those of the Black Parents Movement to White members, discussed in Chapter 2. The issue is entirely about retaining a Black-led and defined movement.

Being a Black supplementary school is not just about having a predominantly Black staff and student cohort. Though Jason does not necessarily see a problem with more students from other groups coming to the school, it remains important to him that there is still a focus on 'African Caribbean history'. Kwame has always invited other groups to various initiatives but only on the proviso that things are done in a 'Black way culturally'. So it is not enough simply to replicate what already goes on in mainstream schools with a set of Black faces. Implicit in these ideas is the belief that there is something different being constructed in the education of Black supplementary schooling, and that the difference is framed in Blackness. It then becomes essential for Black children to engage in a Black education and to learn about their heritage and culture. Other groups are welcome to engage in this education too, but it cannot be at the expense of, or detriment to, the nature of that education.

The importance of the Black-led environment, however, should not be overemphasized for official projects. At an ILEA-funded supplementary school conference in 1987, a delegate commented from the floor that 'some of us wish that there [might one day] be no need for supplementary schools if only the mainstream would do their job properly' (NABSS, 1987: 6). From this perspective the Black-led environment is seen as instrumental while the schools are failing the children, but it is not seen as ideal. According to this view, Black supplementary schooling exists only because the children are being rejected and discriminated against and there is no recognition of the value of the Black environment and curriculum themselves. A more radical conception of supplementary education challenges the values of mainstream education, necessitating Black educational spaces irrespective of the inclusion of the mainstream schools, and here again we can see the key cleavage between official and self-help projects.

Conclusion

Mirza and Reay (2000: 523) are keen to stress that although a segment of the movement has largely been incorporated into the state and aspires to the goals of the mainstream, Black supplementary schools remain 'both radical and subversive'. As Tomlinson (1988: 65) argues, 'supplementary schooling for minority pupils could be seen as undermining the concept of common education for all'. By providing separate spaces for the education of Black children, they challenge the firmly held notions of colour-blindness evident in the approach of state education authorities.

Black supplementary schools have various types of organization and various philosophical commitments, but despite these differences, they are all motivated by the same concern, and it is this that unites them. They work to remedy the mistreatment of Black youth in the mainstream school system and put immense personal effort into seeing that happen. It is their commitment to Blackness, whether manifested in Black politics or simply in providing a predominantly Black environment, that is the motivation behind the projects and the reason we can refer to Black supplementary schools as a movement, no matter how fragmented.

Chapter 4
Mainstream educational discourse in the official projects

The Black supplementary school movement arose as a specific response to a school system that 'perceived and treated as retarded' Black children and deemed Caribbean culture and communities to be unable to raise intelligent children (Carby, 1983: 188). In rejecting this thesis of cultural deprivation, the movement located the cause of the problem as being in the performance of the schools rather than the homes, communities, and minds of Black children. However, as we saw in the last chapter, Black supplementary schools have become increasingly accommodated into the mainstream school system, through funding and accreditation. This chapter briefly examines the role of the Black-led churches, which have become progressively more involved in the provision of supplementary schooling. We see how this increasingly accommodative position has led to the movement adopting the mainstream discourse of cultural deprivation and individualization to tackle the educational inequalities faced by Black children. Underachievement and individualized conceptions of racism now underpin much of the activity of the official Black supplementary school projects.

Black-led churches

Majority Black-led churches have played an important role in Black supplementary education. Errol estimates that the 'majority' of supplementary schools are sustained by churches and many projects in the study had some link to a church. This should come as no surprise as the Black church has been the single largest organization in Black communities in the West since the days of enslavement when church communities were the only permitted arenas for mass meetings of Black people (Dyson, 2000; Pearson, 1978). As already stated in Chapter 1, Barrow observed: 'no other group or individual among us has the authority that the black churchman has and therefore we need authority figures and this is where the black churches come in' (Barrow, nd: 8).

Black supplementary schools did not, however, arise from the church and should be distinguished from Sunday schools, which involve religious instruction. Rather, supplementary schools are located within churches because, as Clive explained, the church is 'responsive' to the needs of the community. Carlton said his supplementary school was started through the 'vision' of the church pastor:

> The church is the bastion for the community. All other organizations have failed. Such as Black councillors, Black organizations that say they're sticking up for Black rights ... The church for Black people, whether you're an African or a West Indian, it's an integral and important part of our society ... I don't think that if this [the supplementary school] were set up anywhere else it would work.

Though there are any number of supplementary schools that have strong relationships with churches, such close support for the movement has not always been as forthcoming from the church. As Nia argued:

> The cooperation from the churches has been pretty poor. There was even a Saturday school where all the children and the parents were going to the nearby church but they had to struggle to pay for a hall. The church was massive. It had 70 departments, a crèche, 24-hour hotline, but the Saturday school was not allowed to use their premises on a Saturday morning when it was empty.

Menelik reported that he had found churches to be 'reluctant' to support the supplementary schools in the early period of the movement:

> Some of the churches wouldn't have Saturday schools ... the church congregation wouldn't support it. It's frightened about being Black and being aware of who you are and having a racial identity so that that was a big problem for a lot of people.

This is not to say that Black churches were against the positive construction of Blackness and community unity. The ideas of Black solidarity and community are at the foundation of the Black church and have sustained it. What some churches have objected to is not Black pride but Black radical arguments that challenge the authority of the state. The Black church has had an antagonistic position in both Britain and the United States towards Black radicalism.

At the height of the Civil Rights movement in the USA, such groups as the Nation of Islam were able to rise to prominence in part due to the perceived conservatism of the Black church. Malcolm X chastised Christianity and branded church leaders such as Martin Luther King as puppets of the state (X, 1965). He argued that the church was the leader of the Negro revolution, going head bowed to the master and begging for fair treatment. The Nation of Islam, he asserted, represented the Black revolution, the 'new type of Negro' who 'makes no apology for his Black skin' and would not be pacified by the White power structure (X, 1971: 91). The veracity of such arguments is irrelevant; it is the vulnerability of the Black church to accusations of conservatism that is important.

The Civil Rights movement showed fierce resistance, marching through the hostile towns of the American South. Yet because of its goals of mainstream success the movement was accommodated into the structures of power. The Civil Rights movement took an approach to resistance that aimed to change the minds of the people in power. Consequently, distinct efforts were made to carry the White population along and to have close relationships with politicians (Dyson, 2000). It is this *accommodative resistance* that drew condemnation from radicals.

Malcolm X (1965: 280) dubbed the showpiece event of the Civil Rights movement, the 1964 march famous for the 'I Have a Dream' speech, the 'Farce on Washington'. He called it a scripted delusion that 'even Hollywood couldn't have topped'. His objection was to the choreographed nature of the event, which was devoid of all spontaneity and tightly controlled to portray a unified message:

> There wasn't a single logistical aspect uncontrolled. The marchers had been instructed to bring no signs – signs were provided. They had been told to sing one song: 'We Shall Overcome'. They had been told how to arrive, when, where to arrive, where to assemble, when to start marching, the *route* to march. First-aid stations were strategically located – even where to *faint*!
>
> (X, 1965: 280–1, original emphasis)

While the accommodative resistance of the Black-led church may not always be so regimented, the story is instructive as it demonstrates the complicated relationship between the church, the Black community, and the state. The model of the Black churches in the Civil Rights movement has been influential for church leaders in the United Kingdom.

The Black church is in a complicated position, as a religious organization holding a political role in terms of representing the community. Black 'leaders' often come from the church and, thanks to their accommodative stance, have the ear of politicians. Being a leader in the community, the Black church requires a political stance and this is authored by its religiosity. This is reflected in Clive's response when asked if it was a problem when the LEA insisted they opened their doors to other groups:

> No no no. If we had been coming from a rigidly Black nationalist perspective that would [have] been an issue, but we're Christians and even if we don't go through the same funding agencies it will be open to the community because [it's] part of the church's outreach. It has to be relevant to the community and so we will help whosoever comes to the door.

The moral stance of the church causes Clive to feel political distaste for a 'Black nationalist perspective'. For Errol too, Christian values are the basis of his organization. Messages of conciliation and forgiveness lead to a relationship with mainstream society predicated on bridging the divide with the mainstream. There is no room for the challenge of Black radicalism, which threatens to destabilize relations with the majority community.

The prevalence of the majority Black-led churches today in the Black supplementary schools determines the approach of much of the sector. They aim to help Black youth to achieve the grades they need to succeed in the school system and in society. That succeeding is desirable is not in question, but access to the system becomes the yardstick by which success is measured. No attempt is made to transform or even challenge the school system, but only to improve the position of Black children within it. It is indisputable that the Black church has been vitally involved in activism (D'Apolitio, 2000). I am not challenging this record, but its fight for rights and justice ultimately aims to support and accommodate mainstream society. Accommodating mainstream goals involves accommodating mainstream ideologies, as clearly indicated by the dominant discourse of Black underachievement.

Underachievement

Underachievement has become the hegemonic frame through which educational inequalities facing African Caribbean students are viewed. Policy makers, researchers, and educationalists have spent years and money trying to solve the problem of this underachievement (Gillborn, 2008). At one level, 'underachievement ... intimates some measure of achievement but not to the degree to which the individual is capable', so it can be seen in a positive sense – the expectation is that Black children can and should succeed (Reeves and Chevannes, 1983a: 38). This is a marked improvement from writing off Black children as being educationally subnormal. However, Reeves and Chevannes reject the term 'underachievement' and argue that it represents a continuation of the cultural deprivation thesis of the deficient Black child and community.

Indeed, a strong theme that emerged from my research was the rejection of the notion of underachievement. Some participants argued that Black supplementary schools were fostering 'overachievement'. In Palsent's view:

> It's not about underachievement now. What we've found is that a lot of the children that come to our school are overachieving. One particular girl we've had to move her up to a higher year group, even though it's not her age. We would do that, but you don't do that in a primary school and secondary school in this country usually. But we move children up if we find that they're achieving very well.

Participants were keen to cite examples that countered the stereotype of the failing Black child. Laying the blame for the failures of the school system at the door of Black pupils is regressive in that it assumes that it is Black students who should be doing better.

The deviant Black person and family, producing children incapable of thriving in school, has been a key figure in the imaginations of those on the Right (King *et al.*, 2001). Charles Murray's infamous take (1990) on the underclass was echoed in Britain. Right-wing commentators blaming Black people is now expected; what is novel and more dangerous is the increasing trend for Black commentators to adopt the same position.

Black blame

Sewell (2009) reflects self-blame when he argues in his book *Generating Genius* that institutional racism is not to blame for the plight of Black students in school. His target for the ills facing the Black community is Black culture and particularly the Black family and its absent fathers:

> If Black boys are disproportionately 'naughtier' in schools than other pupils because they lack the restraining hand of a father then what can we as a community do? These are the tough questions that our community should have faced long ago. Instead, we avoided them. It was too easy to allow liberal scholars and Black nationalists to blame everything White ... Fatherhood and its absence is key to understanding the crisis facing many, though not all, Black boys in the UK ... *we are doing something to ourselves* and too often it happens to be another version of envy and loathing.
>
> (Sewell, 2009: 25, emphasis added)

According to Sewell, Black boys do not succeed in school because they are damaged by the effects of growing up without their fathers, in a community bereft of positive role models. The absence of a father may well have a negative impact on children, and cultural arguments about school success are common (e.g. Modood, 2005). However, it is essential to move beyond seeing negative aspects of an oppressed community's culture as the problem. Rather, we must look at the way negative cultures arise *because* of oppressive conditions. In Britain at least one in five Black men is unemployed (Ramesh, 2012) and Black men are vastly overrepresented in the criminal justice system (ONS, 2004). So it should not be a surprise that there is a problem with Black men supporting their families. But it is a mistake to see absentee fathers as a development of Black culture, as if it were somehow natural.

Sewell does attempt to address the educational success of Black pupils with his Generating Genius programme. However, his flawed philosophy is evident in the practice of the programme, which takes talented African Caribbean boys and exposes them to universities in the UK and the Caribbean. The inherent flaw in the programme is that the 'talented tenth' model can benefit only those deemed 'bright' enough to be the future of the community, so reinforcing the marginalization of the presumably backward ninetieth.

Another foundational problem with Sewell's work is that his analysis and programme are founded on so-called underachieving boys. This is due to his perspective being based on seeing Black familial forms as deviant, and is a common feature of the underachievement discourse that is usually, and incorrectly, based around Black, particularly Caribbean, boys.

Black boys as the problem

Underachievement has commonly assumed that it is Black boys who fail to achieve school success. Participants in the study alluded to the prevalence of this view and two of the projects were specifically focused on Black boys, which is important in the construction of Black underachievement. Young Black men are specific targets of cultural deficit ideology, labelled as aggressive, disruptive, and violent, because male representation is central to how the Black community is pathologized (Cole, 2004).

Howarth describes how the Black male is constructed as 'academically inferior, naturally aggressive, and sexually dangerous' within mainstream discourse (2004: 367). The Black male is endowed with a hyper-masculinity and this is marked as a threat to society. Such a construction finds its roots in slavery and the fear of a Black uprising. The Black, aggressive, sexual creature is animalized and crudely represented as more beast than man (Davis, 1982). This bestial characterization leads to criminalization of the Black male, as was apparent in the moral panic of the myths around mugging in the 1980s (Zack-Williams, 1997). Wilson (1994) argues that the criminalization of the Black male is essential for the majority White population, as it underpins their superiority and status in society. He asserts that White superiority is an essential feature of racist domination, which is in part maintained by pathologizing the Black community. Whatever the case, men certainly dominate the representation of the inner city and the Black community with their 'apathy, recalcitrance, fecklessness, and aggression' (Mirza and Reay, 2000: 526). In this representation of the Black community, females and their more discreet forms of resistance are made invisible. When we think of the Black community we are invited to picture gangs, drugs, and anti-authority Black males.

Only when the focus is on African Caribbean boys does the narrative of the deviant Black family, and in particular the father, have utility. It seems intuitive that no father equals no role model, which in turn equates with bad school performance. However, this entirely ignores the reality that African Caribbean girls are subject to the same patterns of inequality, relative to other girls, as their male counterparts (see Appendix: Figure 1 and Table 1). Since the Black mother is apparently ever present in the household, we cannot explain these results by the absence of a woman on which to model their behaviour and self-esteem. The obsession with the lack of educational success of Black boys works to reinforce the narrative of the failing Black family with the absentee father. This flawed analysis nonetheless provides the favourite panacea of politicians: role models.

Role models

According to the *Guardian* (Muir, 2007), the army and the police were drafted in by the New Labour government to provide role models for disaffected Black young men on the grounds that the youth are not exposed to enough 'successful' people in their communities. Presumably, being introduced to those in the army and police would inspire them to greater heights than even their tower block dwellings. It is deeply problematic to assume that role models are a priority or a cure for solving inequalities in education because the premise is all about changing the boys and not the schools. Sarah, who organized a Saturday school programme from a local university in her city, is the only White person interviewed in the study so we should not take her comments as representative. However, her attitude is emblematic of the role model approach that sees the 'trait' of lack of preparedness and unpunctuality as part of the culture of the Black community:

> Sometimes the trait we're talking about seems to be coming through. Although *we're trying to get role models in for them*, if you've got a teacher there who hasn't got the photocopies, hasn't brought the hand-outs ... if it happens frequently then how much of this is still in the culture and is any progress being made? [emphasis added]

Sarah is perplexed as to why the role models the programme provides are not adequately promoting the values required. The idea that an organization outside of the Black community would need to provide role models demonstrates the extent to which this position is stuck in an ivory tower block, where the Black community is the one we see in movies and rap songs.

The invisibility of Black women becomes extremely significant. African Caribbean women have always been very active in the labour market, as is well documented (Reynolds, 2001). Even if we have given up on feckless Black men, it seems odd that the tradition of the hard-working Black woman cannot provide a suitable place for Black youth to learn how to behave 'appropriately'. Instead, we are left with a community shorn of so-called successful individuals for Black youth to emulate.

The Black community is pathologized within this discourse to the extent that when asked if the supplementary schools would be necessary in the future, Sarah said that the educational gap is narrowing but she cannot be wholly optimistic because:

> The worrying trend is the increase in crime, and the gang issues that seem, as portrayed by the media, to be escalating. I'm always a bit wary of taking what the media says at face value but if that's going to carry on, if that is escalating, then it could mean that in 15 years' time there could still be a need because we've still got groups that are particularly underachieving.

Sarah appears to be arguing that if it were not for the 'escalation' of crime and gangs that is stifling Black achievement, there would be no problems in terms of educational attainment for Black youth. Again, we see a discourse shaped around a deviant male culture (gang life) holding the community back.

Negative descriptions of the Black community came not only from Sarah. Most of the participants in the study alluded to a negative Black culture. For instance, Gloria spoke of the Black youth culture as 'this sort of young people's community, which is I guess you know partly the gangs, partly dabbling with drugs, you've got that kind of community going on.'

Me, myself, and I

Interviewees did not confine their negative descriptions of the Black community to the youth. Parents came in for much criticism for being too busy socializing to pay attention to the education of their children. Kwame was critical of the role of mothers now that the extended family is breaking down:

> Mother operates on what we call a subconscious base, and that means food, clothes, and shelter. The educational aspects, the exposing and stimulating the child at an early enough age, is no longer there, so you find children 0 to 5 who are very bright, but they're not stimulated. They're not preparing the children, they're not preparing work, engaging, and therefore mothers spend a lot not doing, okay there's the issue of mothers going to work as well, but you find that there's not a preparedness of the child for their future.

Kwame regarded mothers as neglecting their duties in order to engage in 'alternatives'. Much of the negativity in the community was embodied within the participants' concerns over increasing individualism. Carlton argued that:

> Black parents, I think that we talk a good shop, where we talk about 'oh we want to give our children the best'. But in reality we don't act that out, we don't do it. We send our children to supplementary school because it's easy for us to go shopping and do other things.

There was a feeling that parents were becoming selfish and people were generally not as willing to give back to their communities as in the past: what Gloria referred to as the 'me, myself, and I mentality'. According to the participants, individualism is to blame for many of the problems in the Black community, including the inequalities in the education system. However, the participants did not describe this as being innate or particular to the Black population but quite the opposite. Rose maintained that things were different in Jamaica, and Gloria traced it back to the legacy of Thatcherism. Black people's experiences in the West are being seen as at the root of the negativity pervading the Black community. Clive said:

> Our community's been devastated by what slavery's done to it and even though they're talking about slavery has been abolished, no it hasn't. The mindset that damaged us is still alive and kicking so we have devastated communities still working out what's been happening.

So when Kwame argued that the Black community has become stagnant and says 50 per cent of it is 'deadstock', he blames the wider society and not Black people. He even identifies the cultural devastation of the Black community as the main reason for lack of respect and Black people not taking responsibility for each other.

In the underachievement discourse, what prevents Black youth from success is the negative experience of their home and community environment. Individualistic solutions are offered: students should work hard, maintain focus, and achieve their full potential. A focus on the individual obstructs any 'serious analysis of institutional structures and educational processes' (Graham, 2001: 61). Yet many participants in the study focused on the self-inflicted problems of the Black community and exhibited individualist concerns for the education of Black youth, rather than anger against the school system.

Individualizing racism

All of the Black participants thought that mainstream schools still had a significant problem with racism but that the nature of the racism had changed, away from the overt to the implicit, what Nia called 'undercover' racism. Sonia suggested that because of this, parents might not see racism in the schools, though it persists:

> A lot of parents wouldn't come along now and say there's racism, but the sort of difficulties that parents have with some children in mainstream schools all points to that. The underlying assumptions are the same. The underlying assumptions are that as Black children they're not intelligent enough, they're not brainy enough, they're not capable enough and that still goes on now, very very sadly … I don't know how much has actually changed.

Alongside being seen as less explicit, the experience of racism was individualized and often said to be the result of specific teachers' prejudice. Angela demonstrates how this dynamic plays out when she discusses institutional racism:

> I mean there's a problem isn't there in the Macpherson report about institutional racism. It's only again, those procedures and policies that the individuals would have designed to help that organization to run. Those are then set up to work more in favour of some … than others, but it's still the individual players who are going to enforce that.

The Stephen Lawrence Report (Macpherson, 1999) was groundbreaking in going beyond the thesis of the Scarman Report of 1982 that racism in the police was due to a few bad apples in the force. Macpherson was the first to acknowledge that institutions such as the police or schools were systematically or institutionally racist. However, we can see from Angela's quote that this systemic racism is still viewed in individual terms; she is arguing that it is the individuals who make the policies who are to blame and not the institutional culture. So if there were non-racist individual policy makers, legislation would cease to be racist. Such individualizing of institutional racism is also dominant within mainstream discourse. The much-watched BBC Documentary *The Secret Policeman* attempted to uncover institutional racism in the police force but drew this conclusion:

> The majority of the officers I met will undoubtedly turn out to be good, non-prejudiced ones intent on doing the job properly. But the next generation of officers from one of Britain's top police colleges contains a significant minority of people who are holding the progress of the police service back.
>
> (Daly, 2003)

Just as institutional racism is assigned to the practice of individual officers in the police force, so racial inequality in schooling is attributed to prejudiced teachers. One of the major complaints from Black communities has been the dearth of Black teaching staff in school. Rose and Henry talked about how Black teachers were excluded in the 1960s:

> *Rose:* It frustrated us when we came to England as teachers and they wouldn't accept our papers that they marked at Cambridge to qualify us as teachers. A lot of us came here and went into factories and that's when Britain made the first mistake. By not taking that group of Black teachers because we say, 'alright Black people are going to England and they're going to have children, and children need Black teachers to sort of help them to settle down in schools', but Britain wouldn't have us.
>
> *Henry:* Well I don't think they made a mistake. It's a deliberate plan, that's my view and it's politics.
>
> *Rose:* They did it deliberately.

This tale of exclusion is reminiscent of the scene in Andrea Levy's 2004 novel *Small Island*, where Hortense, a teacher from Jamaica, is summarily rejected from teaching in the British school system. On the one hand Rose and Henry agreed that Black people were systematically excluded from the teaching profession, an indication of institutional racism. However, the problem they identify works on an individualized understanding of racism. If more Black teachers are the solution, then the problems in the schools are being attributed to the White teaching cohort. The presumption is that if teaching staff did not hold racist views, the problem of racism in schools would be resolved. The same arguments are made about the need to recruit more Black police officers, again based on the premise that racism is located within individuals, and Black people are assumed not to be racist. However, institutional racism indicts systems and not the individuals who are subject to the institutional culture, norms, and values (Carmichael and Hamilton, 1969). If institutions are systemically racist then the colour of the staff is irrelevant; a school would still be institutionally racist even if all of the teachers were Black.

As the low expectations of Black pupils held by White teachers have always been a key criticism of the school system levelled by advocates for supplementary schools, it is clear that these individualistic accounts of racism are prominent within the movement. Another issue marked by individualism is the focus on Black pride.

Black pride and empowerment

A central motivation of the Black supplementary school movement has been to restore the pride in Blackness that was destroyed during slavery and colonialism. Robert Hart (nd: 2) of the West Indian Welfare and Education Association advocated giving the students 'a pride in their Blackness'. And when proposing a platform for the reorganization of supplementary schools, Clinton Sealy argued that the projects needed to instil in the pupils a pride in 'themselves and their race' (1974: 1). Nia declared that 'the most important part is the African History. They need to understand their roots, their history, and their culture to feel better about themselves, and to have a far better outlook on life.'

The absence of Black culture and history in mainstream schools is seen as devastating to the Black child. The Ealing Community Relations Council (nd: 1) declared that 'a child sundered from his family roots and language and atmosphere of his infant years risks psychological damage ("rootlessness") and social damage (exacerbated culture clashes within the family)'.

It is seen as difficult for the Black child to be successful because of this disconnection from themselves. A flyer for a Black supplementary school run by a Methodist Church in Clapham (1982: 1, original emphasis) is illustrative:

> Insufficient positive reinforcement of the black child's self-image within the schools based on racist textbooks and other material REINFORCE A NEGATIVE SELF-IMAGE WHICH IS FOUND IN THE MEDIA AND IN WHITE SOCIETY AT LARGE. If the schools do not offer a positive self-image it is hardly surprising that black youths see themselves as failures before they have even begun.

Empowerment of Black youth has therefore been a mainstay of the supplementary school projects. Errol was keen that the Black youth in his project should 'not be ashamed of their culture' and Menelik said:

> So what we're doing in terms of education is to educate people that there were great scientists, great engineers, great technicians, you know great doctors, and you know great thinkers in our society, great writers.

Instilling pride in the students as Black people was seen as important to counter the negative representations of the majority society. Learning Black history was important for making them aware of the true legacy of people of African descent. This approach is critical of racism at a systemic level, as the racist discourse of society is being challenged. Black children are seen to be disadvantaged by how society portrays them, and by how this portrayal leads to negative outcomes in schooling and life. Such an approach is supported and reinforced by a plethora of Black psychology literature from the United States, such as Amos Wilson's classic *The Developmental Psychology of the Black Child* (1978). According to this perspective, racism is overwhelming the Black child. As indicated by its roots in psychology, there is a strong individualist component to the idea that the problem of school success is about low self-esteem and negative self-image.

The bedrock of the empowerment ideology lies in individuals being able to achieve, no matter what. The major problem presented is the racism in society, but the message is to overcome this. Therefore the barriers to achievement become negative thinking and being held back by other distractions. For example, Rose said of Blackness, 'don't dwell on it, because we need to go forward'. Among the more official supplementary schools, Blackness becomes something that needs almost to be overcome. Blackness brings with it racism, which will stop the progress of the children, so they need to focus and work harder. From this perspective the solution to breaking through the barriers of racism is not the collective expression of Blackness, but an extreme form of individualism that appeals to a conservative ideology.

Hyper-individualism

Individual responsibility is one of the key tenets of a conservative ideology according to which inequality is put down to the decisions and life choices of the less well-off (Evans, 1997). Conservatism was a theme in the interviews. For example, Gloria compliments Margaret Thatcher because 'in terms of telling people [to] get off your backside and go to work, you know, be entrepreneurs, set up your own businesses, make your ideas come to life, I commend her on that'.

In the same breath, Gloria criticized Thatcherism for the selfishness and greed in society today. However, alignment with a conservative approach to the issue of individual responsibility was not uncommon and one of the projects in the programme had strong ties to the Conservative Party. Empowering individuals and increasing self-esteem among Black youngsters are worthwhile aims, but the theme of self-achievement can be damaging to the community when taken to its extreme because the focus is wholly on the individual. There has been a tendency towards a *hyper-individualism* in the Black community in recent years. In this view, Black people are perceived as able to achieve anything, and any failure is down to the individual concerned. I saw this ideology at work in a conference for Black boys – it always seems to be about the boys – where the facilitator urged them to focus on themselves and their achievements, and to forget their friends, whom he clearly assumed to be a negative influence.

Hyper-individualism is driven by the acknowledgement of racism in society, but, importantly, this reality is not seen as an excuse to fail. As Hart of the West Indian Education Association explains, for Black children it is necessary to:

> Make them competitive. Instil in them that to serve in a White man's country and in an alien community, they have to work and study harder in order to be better than the rest. They must know that the opportunities are there, but because they are Black, to get them they must be not merely as good as the White applicant, but a great deal better. This philosophy of life and living must be drilled into them from birth, so that it finally relates not only to sport and academic excellence, but permeates every aspect and facet of their lives.
>
> (Hart, nd: 2)

Thus the response to racism is to work harder, be more focused, and not let anything (or anyone) get in the way of success. This is why self-image is seen as so essential to the school success of Black children. While it is certainly not being argued here that hard work and focus are not positive attributes to aim for, there are significant limitations with the hyper-individual viewpoint. Reeves and Chevannes (1983a: 22) argue that a focus on the individual's own achievement and the barriers to success that they face submerges more 'alternative and more radical solutions'. They contend that:

> By taking for granted that all are striving for the same success, it camouflages educational divisions ... and avoids the question of whether the existing competitive meritocratic system of education can ever ensure equality of educational opportunity.
>
> (Reeves and Chevannes, 1983: 40)

Offering solutions such as building self-esteem to the problem of the inequalities in mainstream schooling fails to challenge the system and the assumptions on which it is based. If the sole answer to the problems of racial inequality in schooling is to get Black children to focus, work hard, and excel, then it is taken for granted that the school system in which they aspire to succeed is appropriate and acceptable. It is over this positioning that the cleavage between the official and the self-help projects discussed in the previous chapter can be seen. The official side of the movement is better accommodated in the mainstream because the only problem it sees with society is the lack of access Black people have to it. The self-help segment, on the other hand, questions the basis of the education that British society produces.

Conclusion

As the Black supplementary school movement has developed it has become increasingly accommodated into the mainstream school system. Inevitably, accommodation has required accepting the broad structures of the school system and some convergence of the ideas of individual responsibility and underachievement embodied in the messages of hyper-individuality. There is good cause for such an approach, as British society remains characterized by the racial inequalities that students must battle, and therefore supplementary schools try to prepare the students to work harder and focus more on achieving. However, radical approaches do exist within the supplementary school movement that challenge the foundation and values of mainstream schooling and attempt to construct alternative spaces of education. These are explored in the next chapter.

Chapter 5
The self-help challenge to the mainstream school system

Ideas of cultural deprivation that characterize mainstream educational discourse are also at work in the conservative official supplementary schools. This chapter begins by examining how the seemingly negative subcultures developed by some Black youth have been explained in reference to the exclusionary culture of mainstream schooling and society. The self-help segment of the Black supplementary school movement retains a fundamental critique of the nature of the mainstream school system and argues that Black young people are in need of African-centred education so that they can challenge the Eurocentric values of individuality and materialism. The chapter discusses this standpoint and considers the approaches to Black, or African-centred, independent schooling. It is argued that though this approach contains radical sentiments, it is essentially an embrace of the same accommodative resistance as is seen in the official projects. Inherent in the entire Black supplementary school movement is both a challenge to, and a reinforcement of, the mainstream school system. Being a minority population makes such apparently contradictory positions the only way to negotiate inequalities, because there is no choice but to engage in the 'master's house' (Lorde, 1984: 110).

Niggativity

As revealed in the previous chapter, a strong theme found in the interviews was that Black youth were seen as susceptible to gangs and criminality. The attraction of 'easy money' through illicit activities was thought to be a strong pull against boring schooling where the benefits might not be seen for years. It almost appeared at times as though there were only two choices for Black youth: either success in school leading to engagement with mainstream society or the rejection of education and descent into the trap of street life. Jason reflected on the construction of street life when he offered the following explanation for the problems with the behaviour of Black youth in schools:

> They're rejecting school because they don't like what's being offered, they're not respected. They're being treated like kids [in school] when at home they're being much more treated like an

adult. Peer pressure, education not being seen as the thing ... easy money through sort of crime, sort of drugs, and whatever else robbery, that type of stuff.

The spectre of the subversive section of the Black population who reject school and society is paralleled in Black communities in the United States. Comedian Chris Rock (2002) became infamous for his diatribe about the civil war going on in the Black community, between the upstanding, hardworking Black people on one side and 'Niggas' on the other. Niggas were said to represent all the negatives of the Black community and to wear stereotypes as badges of honour. The term has also become widely used by Black youth in Britain (Quinn, 2000) and though none of the participants used the actual word in their interviews during the study, the concept of Nigga was ever present.

Nigga is most commonly associated with Gangsta Rap music, with its overt embrace of negative hyper-masculine stereotypes of Black people (LaGroan, 2000). The embrace of Nigga is a direct result of the conditions faced by Black communities trapped in urban ghettos (Young, 2004). Essentially, the hopelessness caused by the conditions they face leads some to reject mainstream society and embrace the culture of the street. Judy (1994) asserts that this experience has deep roots and can be traced all the way back to plantation society and the figure of the Badman who stalked the plantation, striking fear in the hearts of both Black and White.

Positive identification of Blackness has been essential to movements of progress and resistance by Black communities (see Chapter 2), so this embrace of the negative representations of Nigga has appalled some (Upchurch, 1997). In the USA the negative Black culture has been attacked, with African American comedian Bill Cosby lambasting the 'deficient' language, lack of respect, and poor parenting (Dyson, 2005). There is some tendency to see the uneducated mass of Black people as holding back the advancement of the Black population. This creates a tension between those closest to achieving access to the fruits of the system and those furthest away.

The concept of Nigga, however, is defended for its positive attribute of connecting Black people together and for being a tool of resistance to racial domination (Martinez, 1997). This is not the place for a debate over the utility of Nigga or the divisions between the Black poor and middle classes. It is enough to indicate why aggression, violence, lack of respect for authority, and to an extent criminal activity, are adopted by some Black people as *the* way to represent your Blackness. Furthermore, this image of the Nigga has become so pervasive that it is taken as a dominant form of representation of Black youth, even within the community itself.

Oppositional culture

In reaction to the negative stereotypes and identifications, reclaiming Blackness as a source of pride has become a fundamental feature of the Black supplementary school movement. It is almost taken for granted that Black people will simply internalize the negative ascriptions of society, leading to low self-esteem and self-hatred. As Palsent explained:

> We're coming from an environment where there are so many negative stereotypes, the media, there's so much negativity. The achievements are not sufficiently shown in my opinion ... Our children don't always have a lot of confidence, self-esteem is low.

The American study by Clark and Clark (1940) in which Black children showed a preference for playing with White dolls has been generalized to the entire Black population in explanation of their low-status positions. The apparent low self-esteem and self-hatred can be used to explain the emergence of Nigga, when continued bombardment with negative imagery breaks down a person's self-esteem until they come to adopt the negative caricatured image of themselves (Upchurch, 1997).

It has been argued by Ogbu (2004) that Black youth have created an oppositional culture to protect them from feelings of inadequacy due to failure in the mainstream. This oppositional culture is said to be a rejection of mainstream values and an embrace of street life. Embracing the oppositional culture is said to protect the youth from low self-esteem because they are not measuring their self-worth by success in the mainstream. Although the psychological benefits are acknowledged, these oppositional cultures are generally regarded as problematic, as Carlton reflects in interview:

> A child needs to know that, I need to behave in a particular way at school ... If a child can dress in a particular way, behave in a particular way, then what you're going to get is a dysfunctional child at the end of it.

This perspective locates the deficits with the students, and the solution as embracing the dominant culture. The oppositional culture thesis is further flawed by explaining Black forms of expression with reference to White society: Black youth act in one way *because* Whites do not. Black culture is understood through the framework of White society and there is no agency for Black communities. Blackness is reduced to a reaction, one more side effect of the racism of Western society. Therefore, the oppositional culture argument is conservative because it both marks out Black expressive forms as deviant and normalizes the cultures of the dominant.

In the British context, it is simply untrue that the Black cultural forms rejected by the school system are created in opposition to the mainstream. The so-called oppositional culture of Black Caribbean youth is displayed, for example, in a style of walking and the speaking of Patois – behaviour teachers can see as defiant. However, neither of these actions arises solely in opposition to living in an oppressive White society; they are cultural practices from the Caribbean. Carter (2003) maintains that far from creating oppositional culture to challenge school authority, Black youths are expressing legitimate but non-dominant cultural capital. It is the cultural capital of their homes and their communities and, importantly, she argues, this culture is in no way deficient. From this perspective, the problem is not that Black students fail to develop the cultural capital necessary to succeed in the school system. That is an argument reserved for conservative commentators such as Cosby. Carter calls instead for an examination of the cultural norms at the foundation of the school system and how these work to exclude Black youth. She advocates the incorporation of the non-dominant cultural capital of the Black community into the school system in order to create an inclusive education.

Radical sentiments

The more radical segment of the Black supplementary school movement presents a challenge to the notion that the school system can ever deliver the equality expressed in its rhetoric. Schooling is not seen as a force for equalizing society; on the contrary, it is viewed as a method of 'producing and reproducing racial, gendered, and class-based inequalities' (Graham, 2001: 61). School is not the solution to inequalities but a significant part of the problem.

Illich (1973) argues that schooling is a fundamental part of the capitalist social and economic system, as it assigns people roles in society. The role of school is not to educate but to legitimate inequality in society by bestowing credentials on the elite. On the basis of the credentials received in schools, people are set into their particular place in society, creating a qualification system that has little to do with education. Far from being a potentially liberatory institution, school reinforces the inequalities in society. It is well documented that certain groups, particularly the poor, are far less likely to gain qualifications. For Illich, this is no accident – it is designed to maintain the necessary balance within society. Similar arguments about the role of school in socializing particular groups into segments of the occupation scale have been made in Britain, for example, by Willis (1977).

The self-help challenge to the mainstream school system

Freire (1985) sees not only the values but also the knowledge of the school system as imbued with the values of the dominant society. He argues that knowledge is produced from the esteemed centres of higher learning, and carries the values of the elite. Knowledge is passed down through the schools and there is no interaction from either teachers or students, who merely receive the rarefied information. Education in this sense is simply about which students can best receive this knowledge without challenging or interacting with it. This process reinforces dominant codes and privileges the privileged.

In the United States, it has been argued that the education system is geared towards reproducing the oppression of the Black community (Seale, 1970). In Britain, Dove has argued that 'schooling ... is a means of perpetuating racialized social relation of power' (1993: 431). As a state institution the school has had a difficult relationship with the Black community; Stone (1981) refers to it as a 'colonizer'.

So one of the major benefits of Black supplementary schools is the Black-led environment (see Chapter 3). 'Comfortable' is how one participant in the study described the environment of the supplementary school for Black students, as opposed to their mainstream experience. The comfort the Black supplementary school provided was a strong theme in the interviews, whereas mainstream school could be seen as alienating. Angela describes how things were in the past and are to some extent today:

> Caribbean people still like to buy their sweet potato, buy their green banana, because that's part of what makes you feel comfortable ... So when the children went to school, the school meals and all these things were alienating to them. They didn't see any Black person who they could talk to and say 'what's happening here?' So it was a totally alienating environment, which must have hindered their ability to sit down in [the] classroom and, really say, 'ah, I'm going [to] really try and learn as much as I can' about the myopic English geography.

The food offered reflects the culture of a school and can reinforce alienation. The detrimental effects on Black students of the hidden and implicit school culture have been discussed in Britain and the United States (see Carter, 2003; Figueroa, 1991). The Eurocentric curriculum in British schools, as mentioned by Angela, is strongly criticized by, among others, Figueroa (*ibid.*). Providing an appropriate educational experience for Black pupils is central to Black supplementary schools. Chevannes and Reeves are unequivocal that 'it is not possible to supplement what does not exist' (1989: 147).

The Black supplementary school movement is inherently critical of the hidden curriculum embedded within mainstream schools. It drives the need to create Black-led spaces of education. However, the movement as a whole does not represent an embrace of radical educational practice that is set on transforming the education system. From remarks such as Angela's we can see that much of the criticism is directed at the cultural level, at how the monoculture of the school system excludes Black children. This is somewhat reminiscent of the 'saris, steel bands, and samosas' criticism levelled at a multicultural education that focused on culture rather than on challenging racist structures in the schools (Troyna and Williams, 1986: 24). The matter of the curriculum can be seen as an extension of the cultural argument, in that Black students need to learn about Black issues because it is part of their culture. This again connects to the question of self-image and esteem. If seen in this light there is not a particular problem with how the school is organized, and the responsibility can be passed to the communities from which the children come.

There is a strong history of supplementary schooling in Britain (Hall *et al.*, 2002; Issa and Williams, 2009). As Lorraine said:

> All cultures that have set foot in this country, Chinese, Polish, Japanese, Albanian, Greek, Jews, whoever they have all set up their schools to preserve their culture and their heritage because they did not see that as the business of the mainstream schools.

A focus on Black history and culture need not represent a challenge to the state, as shown by the Descendants supplementary school. In a recent book about their experiences, Mahoney and Noel (2012: 7) explain that their project is:

> An arts-focused educational project. During the weekly sessions our main focus is on African and Caribbean culture; we explore history, we experiment with art, craft, music, drama, and dance. We encourage young people to develop a sense of pride in their abilities through increasing their self-confidence.

The Descendants is extremely African-centred and uses arts to cover all areas of Black history including enslavement, but this African-centredness is not meant as a rejection of mainstream schooling or society. Mahoney and Noel's book proudly showcases how the supplementary school has been endorsed by figures such as Diane Abbot, MP. The students met Tony Blair when he was Prime Minister, and even the Queen, when they performed at her Jubilee celebrations. The Descendants project achieved the highest award from the supplementary school accreditation body ContinYou, confirming that it has blended its African-centredness with an approach endorsed by mainstream organizations.

Stone (1981: 174) argued that 'Saturday schools are tolerated so long as they appear to be fulfilling a specific need' for the state. This is why the state eventually embraced Black supplementary schools, realizing that many of the projects did not seek to challenge their role but to support it. There has, however, been a trend within the movement that has proposed a thorough overhaul of the process of schooling for Black children.

African-centred education

Much of the focus on learning Black history was on an attempt to raise the self-esteem of the students as Black people. For example, the Peter Moses Supplementary School (nd: 1) asserted that Black history was important 'to bring to the attention of the pupils the contribution which Black people have made through the ages and in so doing to assist in raising their self-image'. However, a section of the self-help corner of the movement challenges the values of the mainstream schools for being Eurocentric. As Dove (1993: 431) states:

> Anyone aspiring to and believing in the same European-centred cultural value system will undermine and devalue the potential for Africans to appreciate African self-worth and self-development as a basis for self-determination.

Dove is arguing that the cultural values of the school are characterized by Eurocentrism and it is this that is holding back Black youth. The critique of Eurocentric education in the UK follows literature from the USA. Hilliard (1998: 115) is among many who argue that:

> For four centuries Africans have endured overt white supremacist beliefs and behaviours. The schools have been and continue to be a structure of domination of Africans by Europeans, through curriculum, school culture, methods of instruction, and public policy.

Hilliard asserts that the only way to counter this Eurocentrism that is poisoning the minds of Black youngsters is to create an African-centred education based on a different set of values. African value systems are contrary to the 'goals of most educational systems in the Western culture', which are 'essentially selfish and materialistic' (*ibid.*: 10). For Hilliard it is necessary to embrace more communal understandings of education and society based on traditional African principles:

> Education, to our ancestors, was regarded as a social rather than an individual process. Serious efforts were taken to establish the social bonds necessary to create a cohort of learners who were not only students, but who would be lifelong brothers and sisters in the most profound sense of those words.
>
> (*ibid.*: 11)

The values of communal learning are essential for transforming how Black children view the world. They are aimed at connecting the students to an understanding of African spirituality, which Hilliard believes will transform their world view and the African Diaspora as a whole. When interviewed, Lorraine explained the importance of embedding African values in schooling:

> Every people and culture brings something to the world and I think our one is something to do with humanity, being the first people ... There is something very unique about how people get along with each other. The patience and the understanding and the wisdom that they bring to human relationships I think is quite profound ... If we have a school it would need to be rooted in that philosophy, *Ubuntu*, which recognizes this deep interrelatedness of people and is not just I am on my own and pull myself up by my bootstraps and kick everybody else.

So Black supplementary schools have not emerged merely to help Black children achieve better results in mainstream schools but to exemplify how the Black community has 'been engaged in a struggle to redefine what constitutes education' (Carby, 1983: 183). Menelik is a strong advocate of an African-centred education, because he believes learning plays a powerful role in shaping people. For example, on the leadership in Africa he has this to say:

> The leadership in Africa is so confused because they don't even know who they are and that's really unfortunate for us because their education is the Western education. They have a European mindset; they don't have an African mindset.

'African education', as he puts it, is not solely focused on learning information and skills but also on teaching values such as 'respect', 'non-violence', and 'fulfilment'. Education is seen much more broadly than as a matter of gaining qualifications, but holistically, in the sense that it is central to a person's development. An African-centred education was by no means the mainstay of the practice of supplementary schools, but the idea of Black youth needing a specialized educational programme was a recurrent theme.

In the call for an African-centred education we see a reimagining of the purpose and process of schooling. The aim is to provide a new value basis, a new lens for looking at society that will transform the minds of a generation of children and consequently have a transformative effect on how they shape the future. This kind of political education is reminiscent of the Liberation Schools of the Black Panthers (see Chapter 3), where the purpose was to mould future revolutionaries. African-centred education is, however, significantly different in its focus on the cultural rather than the overtly political.

African-centred education is predicated on a political critique of Eurocentric instruction, highlighting the role of the MAAFA (enslavement) and continued oppression of the African mind (Hilliard, 1998). Essentially it presents the psychological argument based on self-image that I discuss in Chapter 4. The solution to the problems facing Black communities is to embrace African history and values, so as to free the mind. Once this is achieved Black people can create their own destinies. Unlike the Black Panther approach, in the African-centred paradigm the re-education and saving of the mind *is* the process of revolution – thereafter all else falls into place. There is no politics of revolution (or social transformation) that comes with African-centred education. The solution is the embrace of an alternative culture of Africaness. However, 'culture is crucial to revolution, but it is not revolution' (Warren, 1990: 26), and without a political framework for change, African-centred education concentrates on individuals, getting them to adopt African culture and values. While this process inherently critiques mainstream schooling, the focus on culture and values does not radically challenge schooling. Perhaps this was why there was widespread support for the creation of Black independent schools from those I interviewed on both sides of the official/self-help divide.

Black independent schools

Black supplementary schools have been offering alternative provision to mainstream education for over 40 years. The continued demand for this provision could suggest that a more complete Black education is necessary for Black children. Lorraine stated that 'tinkering at the sides on a Saturday is not enough' and strongly advocated the creation of full-time schools with a different ethos from the mainstream. Much of the support for Black independent schools stemmed from the belief in the need for a focus on Black issues in the curriculum. Gloria explained her support for Black schools:

> I just think if we have any hope of our young people getting back to really understanding who they are, because right now they are completely lost, they don't see where they fit in, they really don't, now if they don't know their worth their value and their purpose, how are we going to get them to succeed? I strongly believe that we should have some Black schools.

Gloria believes Black children are lost in the mainstream schooling system and that a Black school would ground them. They would have a place to fit in there:

> I think in terms of the school ethos, as well as delivering the curriculum and making sure that they're attaining what they should do, I think the cultural element of it, that understanding of who they are, the sense of pride and I guess, you would then create a community, where you'd, you'd look at how you treat each other.

Gloria asserts that the youth need to be able to appreciate their Blackness if they are truly to understand themselves, and she does not believe that this can be achieved in the mainstream schools. The Black, or African, environment constructed would enable Black young people not only to connect to the school but to build a positive sense of self and build better relationships with each other.

So the call for Black independent schools was not always radical. Everyone who supported the idea was clear that attainment in mainstream exams would be an essential focus. Having a more inclusive school, which included teaching Black history and culture, would aid mainstream attainment. As Sonia explains, the two are compatible:

> We know what we mean when we say a Black school. In other words, we're wanting a school that is predominantly based on our culture, in the same way that other people have their own schools based on their culture, but it doesn't stop them from doing the national curriculum, the important academic-type work that you need to do if you want to make a way in the world.

Black independent schools in the United States have boosted mainstream achievement (Pollard and Ajirotutu, 2001), and this evidence was drawn on by participants. However, some rejected the notion of Black independent schools because they objected to a separationist philosophy. The idea of separating the children on grounds of colour was seen as undesirable, and

The self-help challenge to the mainstream school system

concerns about those of mixed heritage were raised. Errol saw separateness as equated to some schools in the USA that were all-Black and failing:

> We don't believe all-Black schools are the way forward. You know that's like saying every Black school in the Bronx works. We know it doesn't because we've done the research … some areas where probably 90 per cent of the kids are Black … For race relations and all the rest of it it's a non-starter and then you find those schools become ghettoized.

The all-Black environment is not what the advocates of Black independent schools argue will lead to better outcomes. There are certainly schools in the UK that are predominantly Black but these are usually failing schools in disadvantaged areas. Though these schools are Black in terms of the population, they remain Eurocentric in terms of their philosophy, organization, and curriculum. Black schools, or African-centred education, demand a complete rethink of how the schools operate. As Lorraine said:

> We have majority Black schools, walk around any part of London. So it's not just the presence of Black children, it is the presence of the culture, ethos, and framework of that place. In other words, what energy and spirit that it sends out and the teachers and students that it attracts who are coming to rediscover that great part of themselves and make that manifest and in that process uplift those people who right now are at the bottom of the bottom.

For those who supported the independent schools, a Black school would be no different from a religious school in the sense that it has a particular ethos and message drawn from and targeted at a certain group. Those of mixed heritage are included because of their Blackness, their African ancestry. Blackness as a category is not so inflexible that it cannot include hybrid forms (see Chapter 2). The fear of separateness looms over the discussion of Black independent schools as though those pushing for their creation are aiming to create a contemporary apartheid. However, in the conversations with those supporting Black independent schools there was no mention of making separate schools compulsory for Black students and segregating all schools. Black independent schools were spoken of as being an option some people might find useful, providing, in Jason's words, a 'mixed bag of education'. There was also no suggestion of completely excluding other groups. It was about targeting Black youth and having them as the mainstay, as Palsent said:

> If you want a Black-led school or a culturally aware African school, great, but you have to bring in different people, White people, Asian people. I don't think it's an issue of saying you're Black so you can come and you're White you can't.

My interviewees were also keen to stress that the alternative form of education taught in an African-centred school would be useful not only for Black students but for all – that everyone in society could benefit from the values of the schools. Lorraine's vision for African-centred education is for it to be:

> So unique and appealing and so successful there will be people lining up to come. I think that is the key. In the same way that dotted all over the African continent you have British schools, you have American schools where Africans are killing themselves to get in.

There is a potential for Black independent schools, or African-centred education, to develop a vision for mainstream schooling. This may sound counterintuitive given the fear of separateness that pervades the community cohesion agenda entrenched in government discourse. Yet Black supplementary schools, which had a difficult time gaining acceptance by the state, are now fully recognized as a legitimate extension of schooling. In this journey to recognition we may possibly locate the future role for independent schools.

A Home Office Circular informing of the Urban Aid programme (1973: Annex D) indicates the early move by the state to recognize 'the role of the school as a focal point of community activities is one of the central themes of "educational priority"'. A policy of embedding the school within local communities developed, with New Labour promoting the idea of Extended Schools in the Education Act of 2002. The aim has been to open up the schools to their local communities, thus encouraging local people to see the schools as partners. This shift in emphasis was felt by the supplementary schools, which were able to apply for educational funds and create links with maintained schools, and, importantly, use their premises, as Sonia describes:

> The schools opened up a bit more now anyway. For a start it is also a way of them getting some money (laughs). That sounds really terrible, but schools can do their own thing now. I know some schools that let out part of the schools now where people can hold church services; they can hold weddings, parties, and things like that. Schools are a lot more open now because it's just like an ordinary hire. Now we hire parts of the school to run the classes.

Building on this move to embed state schools within local communities, at least rhetorically, the Conservative-led Coalition government has introduced Free Schools as a flagship policy since taking office in 2010. These schools can, in theory, be started by any parents or community groups and the rhetoric is that they empower parents and communities to shape their educational choices. As Schools Minister Lord Hill (DfE, 2011: np) proclaimed:

> For too long, politicians in Westminster have assumed they know best and that more political control means better results. The opposite is true. Good schools know better than politicians how to run their own affairs and that's why we're confident these free schools – which give them real independence – will offer local children a great education.

A critique of the flaws of this rhetoric and the legislation is not given here. The importance for the present argument is that the Free Schools legislation allows for community groups to set up schools that are not subject to the controls of the national curriculum or local education authority. By breaking down these barriers the Conservatives have, somewhat ironically, introduced the possibility of state-funded Black independent schools.

The opportunity this legislation presents has not been lost on activists in the Black community. Lorraine reports that she is aware of at least nine African-centred applications to set up Free Schools, but that all nine were turned down. Though the state is allowing community and parent control of education in some instances, it appears that this will be the case only when the vision of the proposed schools matches that of the government. It is possible and, in light of the ideology of the Conservative Party, highly probable, that the idea of African-centred education does not resonate with the present government. However, given the nature of African-centred education, it is also not unimaginable that the government will find a place for Black schools in the future. African-centred education differs from mainstream schooling in that it is based on African cultural values stressing community and spirit. These would not be radical liberation schools. The goals remain success in life and high achievement, and, when aligned to the hyper-individualistic trend, could present a self-help ideology that connects well with Conservative politics.

In the master's house

Facing African-centred, and more radical, conceptions of education is the problem that Lorde described as using the 'master's tools' to carve our way in their 'house' (1984: 10). Because we reside in Britain – the house – we are forced to engage with mainstream society, even if we accept that it is oppressive. What African-centred education does is attempt to fashion our own tools – education. However, this does not deal with the issue of remaining trapped in the master's house. Radical groups such as the Black Panthers wish to cause a revolt that will tear down the society so it can start again, but they are in a minority, so there is little hope of such revolution. African-centred education seeks solace in achieving success, using an alternative communal value base that, it is hoped, will lead to transformations in the people and therefore society.

That some of those who run supplementary projects object to Black independent schools highlights the dilemma facing minority groups in any society. Even though we may acknowledge that separate institutions are necessary – i.e. supplementary schools to provide educational experiences specific to Black children – we feel it necessary to disavow the next logical step of independent schools as being too radical and separatist. If Black youth benefit from the experience of a Black environment and curriculum in a supplementary school, surely they would benefit from the experience in a full-time arena? This would also allow greater access to more young people in the community.

Conclusion

A strong theme emerged throughout my research: a negative subculture of street life existed that threatened to consume Black youth if they were left marginalized in the school system. This fear was not always interpreted according to the individualistic cultural deficit models examined in Chapter 4. A tradition exists in the Black supplementary school movement that presents a serious challenge to the values at the heart of the mainstream school system and its exclusionary effects on Black youth. Various projects have consequently sought to provide an environment and learning experience that is based on different cultural values deemed appropriate for Black young people. It is these perspectives that have originated the call for Black, or African-centred, independent schooling.

At the same time as criticizing the value basis of mainstream education, however, the African-centred approach in supplementary schools retains faith in the goals of the school system and does not present a radical alternative. Full-time African-centred schools may yet be funded by a Conservative government in the near future. These seeming contradictions are in part because of the diverse nature of the philosophies behind different projects, but they are due also to the position of Black people in Britain. To succeed, it is necessary to engage in mainstream society – even when institutions are

The self-help challenge to the mainstream school system

racially biased. This reality has shaped the accommodative resistance of Black supplementary schools and Black education in general, which is at once a subversive challenge to the mainstream, while simultaneously supporting the system by promoting success within it.

Part Two

The Lumumba School Study

Chapter 6
Researching the Lumumba School

Background

In Part One of this book I presented the literature, archival data, and analysis of in-depth interviews to illustrate the motivations, principles, and ideological tensions that drive the Black supplementary school movement and to capture the key developmental shifts. Part Two presents a study of the process of Black supplementary schooling through the focus on a single ethnographic case study, conducted over seven months, of the Lumumba Saturday School.

The Lumumba Saturday School is the pseudonym I have given to one of the oldest Black supplementary schools in Britain, which dates back to the late 1960s. It was started by a group of young people in the area who wanted to help Black children to succeed in education despite the endemic racial inequalities in the school system. The Saturday School is part of the Uhuru Organization (also a pseudonym), which is committed to Pan-Africanism, and this informs the ethos of the Lumumba School and the centrality of African history and culture in the curriculum.

The programme is based on what Stone (1981) would define as 'self-help'. Though it has received nominal funds from the local education authority in the past, it is not dependent on state funds and is therefore unaffected by changes in state priorities, unlike other programmes in the city. A nominal fee of £2.50 per week per child is charged as a contribution to the materials in the school so that low-income families can afford to send their children. The school runs from 10 a.m. until 2.30 p.m. every Saturday in term time, and takes children of all ages, though those who attended during the research period were typically between the ages of 4 and 12. At the time of the research, the Lumumba School was a small project with a maximum of 12 children attending in any week and four members of staff in all, including myself as the researcher.

We have seen that Black supplementary schools have a diverse range of forms, philosophies, and sizes and so the Lumumba School cannot represent the entire movement. An in-depth analysis of any Black supplementary school might highlight issues and tensions within other projects over, for instance, retaining volunteers, discipline, and parental relationships. There are three primary reasons why I chose the Lumumba School for my study.

First, the project is one of the longest-running Black supplementary schools, dating back to the late 1960s. This heritage allowed me to examine how historical changes have influenced the programme.

Second, its self-help nature was important. There is very little literature on self-help projects, but it is vital to examine how they are organized and sustained, and to determine how the pedagogies and ideologies differ from those deemed more official. Official projects focus on mainstream achievement and are in the process of being incorporated into the mainstream school system, as we have seen. The nature of self-help projects and how they evolved and exist in contemporary Britain, however, requires a different kind of analysis due to the difficulties with accessing this part of the movement.

The self-help nature also allows for fuller appreciation of the changing role of the state in relation to the movement over the years. While the official projects have had some local and national state funding, the self-help projects have received less attention. For example, the fact that the Lumumba School received nominal funding from the LEA for a time is remarkable considering the history of conflict and raises the question of whether self-help projects have changed in order to be incorporated into state funding or whether the view of the state has altered.

Third, and most importantly, is the political foundation upon which the Lumumba School is founded, with its links to the Uhuru Organization. Within the Black supplementary school movement there have been attempts to create curricula and pedagogy that challenge mainstream values and practice. The Lumumba School is one such programme with a long history of this type of endeavour; it therefore provides the perfect site for exploring how radical ideas are taught within the movement. Black supplementary schools are of interest as potential spaces for the production and reproduction of an independent education based on Black, or African-centred, principles. Conducting the ethnography in the Lumumba School allows for a broad interrogation about the value basis of Black supplementary education.

The history and self-help nature of the Lumumba School make it the perfect case to analyse the issues and tensions within the Black supplementary school movement. Analysis of this specific case relates to the discussion and history explored in Part One of the book. It shows how what was experienced in the Lumumba School should influence understandings of Black supplementary schools more generally.

The research process
In order to carry out the study I volunteered as a teacher in the Lumumba Saturday School for seven months, from December 2008 to July 2009. I became part of the school and interacted with other volunteer teachers, students, and parents. How my experiences relate to the discussion of the Black supplementary school movement forms the basis of the empirical study.

The participants in the research were the students and staff at the project, along with the parents. All were given pseudonyms. No inducements were offered to participants in the research process but I did donate £250 of my research funds to the school. The purpose of the donation was not to gain access, as I am sure this would have been granted anyway. My aim was to do research that could benefit the community in general, and the Lumumba School in particular, so making a donation was an irrefutable way to have an impact.

Role of the university
Engaging as a university researcher with Uhuru and other radical community organizations had, in the past, aroused suspicion. 'Student', 'PhD', and 'university' are not always words of currency. More than once I had to justify my wish to be involved in academia, since Black organizations have good reason to be suspicious of it (West, 1993). To understand the concerns of an organization committed to a radical critique of mainstream schooling it is necessary to consider the role of universities in society.

Universities are authoritative because they sit atop the ladder of education. In a radical analysis, Freire (1985) argues that because so-called authentic knowledge is produced by elites in academia, it is repressive to the masses and is designed to maintain the status quo. Therefore, if school systems are racist and detrimental to the Black community, then universities must also be so, as they produce the knowledge that schools teach. Consequently, radical organizations reject the ivory tower of the university and academic research. Numerous authors have called for a greater public involvement by universities to bridge the gap between academia and the community (most notably Burawoy, 2005), but for radicals the problem is not the lack of universities' involvement – rather it is the opposite: they reject the role the university plays in society.

When devising my research method I began with Howard Becker's (1967) famous question: 'whose side are we on?' The wider critique of the role of the university influenced my decisions but it was beyond my control. My aim was to conduct my research in a way that placed me firmly on the side of those in the Black supplementary schools so that I could gain comprehensive insights into the movement.

Due to my commitment to a Black radical analysis of endemic racism in schools and the need to produce an alternative and challenging curriculum, teaching in the Lumumba School was a logical approach. My role as a researcher was clear and I was representing the university. But I was at the same time a concerned member of the community who believed in the ethos of the school and wanted to help out. I was motivated not only to engage in research but to align myself with the Saturday School, its volunteers, parents, and students. My being in both positions raises issues about the research process and reflexivity – questions that have been debated in the history of ethnography.

Ethnography and education

Ethnography requires the researcher to immerse him or herself in the lived experience of the community of study. Insights are gained from being both a participant and an observer in the routine practice of the lives of a researched group. Preissle and Grant (1998) explain how the aim of ethnographic practice is to explore human agency in a research setting. This is in opposition to a focus researching the monolithic structures of society that prevail in much research. Ethnography is often interested in the lived experience, not the theoretical analysis of systems. The work looks at specific locations and tends to restrict knowledge claims to those specific sites, which in educational settings are generally classrooms. Ethnography is therefore open to the criticism that as it is restricted to an individual site it cannot be useful as a critique of wider systems. In fact, much ethnographic work, and its theoretical basis, would not only argue against the idea of systemic critique but would seek to avoid such dialogue (Noblit, 1984). It may, therefore, seem odd to employ ethnography for a research study grounded in the notion of systemic racism. However, ethnography disconnected from theory has been challenged by critical theorists in the creation of what is termed by Anderson 'critical ethnography'(1989: 249). Anderson recounts the debate between the critical theorists and ethnographers in education and sums up the disagreements as follows:

> Critical theorists in education have tended to view ethnographers as too atheoretical and neutral in their approach to research. Ethnographers have tended to view critical theorists as too theory driven and biased in their research.

The aim of critical ethnography is to bridge the gap between structure and agency, and to use the findings of ethnographic research to inform broader structural theory. Anderson cites Willis's (1977) study of working-class children in Wolverhampton as an example. Willis's study was a neo-Marxist exploration of the role of schools in the reproduction of class positions, and used the experience of the students in the school to explore how this process occurred. As Nayak (2006: 412) observes:

> Ethnographies remain delicate cultural constructions intricately interlaced through a diverse community of tellers, listeners, writers, and readers who in turn may unravel and string together these 'truth regimes' differently.

Willis was able to use insights from the 'cultural constructions' of his particular location to inform overarching class theory. The need for ethnography to be atheoretical and largely descriptive (Hammersley, 1985) is justified only by the ideological position that places the role of the academic as separate and outside of the wider community. What Willis did was to take a different, Marxist, ideological position that places the researcher with the researched and therefore uses the insights in a dialectical relationship to his own understandings of society, as has also been done in feminist research (Anderson, 1989).

The politics that inform my research are based on an embrace of Blackness in connection to the African Diaspora and a comprehensive critique of the mainstream school system. One of the major failings of critical theory in the West is that it has been wed to the processes and structures of mainstream institutions. Anderson (1989: 257) acknowledges this limitation thus:

> A persistent criticism of educational critical theory is its tendency toward social critique without developing a theory of action that educational practitioners can draw upon to develop 'counter-hegemonic' practice in which dominant structures of classroom and organizational meaning are challenged.

The school has consistently been the site of critical ethnography and there have been few plausible plans of action for the classroom that could allow for changes in the system presented, which is unsurprising when the classroom is a site controlled by the school system. If the system is set to reproduce inequalities, counter-hegemonic activity can hardly be expected to develop inside its institutions. Local sites may be useful for generating theory about systemic issues, but it is another matter to expect these local sites to produce radical practice that subverts the values of the institution. Certainly, individual teachers have the ability to be innovative, but the extent to which they can do so is limited by the school and the wider system. It is an unrealistic notion that the route to institutional reform will be found in localized innovative practice emanating from particular sites to transform the entire system. Self-help supplementary schools, however, do present potential alternative spaces for contestation of the values and practice of the mainstream schools.

Being actively engaged in the process of the Lumumba Saturday School provided unparalleled access to and understandings of how the Saturday School works and how Blackness is used to frame the practice and purpose of what goes on. The research is dialectical, with my understandings being informed and challenged by my experiences and discussions with people in the Lumumba School. The insights gained from this particular location are used to interrogate and develop the theory and discussions presented in Part One of this book. The goals of this piece of research are to support the Lumumba School, to discover ways to sustain other programmes, and also to evaluate the future of the movement located in such spaces.

Research diary

I present the bulk of my findings as an edited research diary. Fieldnotes in ethnographic research are particularly important as they represent the immediate view of the researcher (Creese *et al.*, 2008). I noted the main happenings in the days I worked there and also my thoughts on wider issues. I could have followed the traditional method of drawing out the themes in the data but because of my epistemological claims that would have been inappropriate. When analysing interviews and focus groups I would not hesitate to use a thematic approach to try to understand participants' talk, as was done with the interviews used for Part One. In these circumstances there is a practical issue involving the amount of data, but more importantly a thematic guide is essential when trying to make sense of others' interpretations of a particular issue (Smith *et al.*, 2009). This could equally apply to participant observation, if the data was meant to work as an analysis of others' interactions. Central to my methodological and epistemological approach is that I present my interpretation of the experience and interactions with others. I stand in a dialectical relationship with the theory and practice of Black education and supplementary schools and my insights form the basis of the research. No attempt is made to represent the experiences and views of others.

Consequently there are no quotes from the participants intended to represent their world view (Back, 2007). No formal interviews were conducted because I was interested in experiencing the process of Saturday school as authentically as possible and reporting the interpretations of my experiences. Inevitably, the process of being a researcher altered the interactions between me and the parents, teachers, and students. However, this changed over the course of the research, to the point where though my role may have been different from that of the other teachers, it was accepted as normal within the school. My relationship with Kamili, one of the teachers, illustrates this. When the research was first explained to her, she was concerned about me 'writing things down' or 'doing experiments', and our relationship was standoffish. However, by the end of the research I considered her a friend and we talked comfortably about all sorts of issues. To introduce formal interviews would have restricted the development of such relationships and therefore my experiences in the school.

Using fieldnotes as the empirical data therefore proved to be the correct methodology. The fieldnotes themselves are accounts filtered through my eyes. To thematically code and present the information neatly packaged filters the data further. I am presenting the empirical material in this way to help readers understand what went on and to show how events affected my thoughts. I am also keenly aware of issues of reflexivity (Milner, 2007). This is vitally important in a dialectic piece as the research diary is a discussion with myself, influenced by experiences and events. The presentation of the diary provides what Lincoln and Guba (1985) call 'thick descriptions' that allow the readers to see the context and understand the development of my ideas in relation to theory and action. I have tried to submit accounts that 'theorize as they describe and describe as they theorize' (Back, 2007: 21), as the experiences are constantly linked back to the theory. Presenting the most complete account of my experiences opens up my ideas to fuller scrutiny and allows the analytical as well as the political to be more seriously challenged.

The following chapter is an edited version of the research diary I kept during my research at the Lumumba Saturday School. There is no pretence of objectivity or affected neutrality. What is presented is an account of my interpretations of the experiences of teaching in a self-help Black supplementary school in line with the wider theoretical discussions outlined in Part One of this book.

Chapter 7
The Lumumba Saturday School
An ethnographic study

Meeting to set up my involvement, 2 December
After my earlier experiences with people in the Uhuru Organization I was slightly apprehensive about the initial meeting to request setting up the research project. At one event I attended I was explaining my Masters research to one of the elders in the organization and he accused me of being a spy for the White man because of my attachment to a university. My motives and intentions attracted suspicion because of my role as a researcher. Because sociology has a history of pathologizing Black communities, it is understandable that academics are sometimes seen as agents of the state. Self-help projects, as organizations that lie outside and challenge the remit of the state, have good reason to be wary of authorities who may wish to shut them down.

It was against this backdrop that I approached Menelik, who runs the Uhuru Organization, about my research proposal. Having spoken to him in the past I knew he would be receptive to research, but I anticipated that he might find the idea of me collecting information while teaching in the programme problematic. I was careful to explain that I wanted mainly to help the project and work as a teacher, in addition to using the school as a case study for my research on the movement. We spoke for about half an hour and he was very receptive to the idea.

My first lesson in reflexivity came from this meeting. My experience of Menelik had been that he was open to research; in fact, he had previously talked to me about the number of people who came to him for interviews. I have even met people at the university whom I would not have imagined would have been welcome but who had been given access to the organization. However, all this experience was overridden by the idea that a Pan-African organization would not be open to the idea of in-depth university research.

Stone (1981) assumes that self-help Saturday schools are closed to the state because they prefer to be accountable to no one. However, being wary of the state and its agents is not about wanting to be unaccountable, merely to maintain independence. Menelik was open to listening to my ideas for the research, and when I explained the motives behind it and my desire to help I was welcomed into the school. I should have expected nothing less.

Kehinde Andrews

First Saturday School experience, 6 December
My elder sister and I had discussed going to help out at the Lumumba School for a few weeks but were not sure what to expect. We went and looked for Menelik, but he was not there so we were led up to the school by a parent who was also a teacher there. When we got upstairs the assistants welcomed our offer of help. We introduced ourselves, said we wanted to help, and took it from there. The Saturday School takes place in one room, with students sharing the space. There were eleven students and three assistants apart from us. I was surprised by the set-up. There did not seem to be much connection with the rest of the organization. The room was up a long flight of stairs and was self-contained, with a bathroom. The teaching space and supplies were all in the one room.

I had expected a well-structured and regimented programme of learning, but no one seemed to be in charge. We discovered that the person who had been running the school had recently left. A volunteer named John had stepped in to take charge and he handed out the work to the students. We were introduced to the children, but beyond that were left to engage as we thought best. There was no discernible structure. Students of different ages and skill levels all sat around one table, doing different pieces of school curriculum work.

The room, which was not very big, was covered in posters of Black pride and history, displaying pictures of Africa and Black heroes. There were a lot of books about Black history but also textbooks, and they were using some photocopies of worksheets from school curriculum materials. There were many potential resources to use for teaching Black history and culture and also for supporting the work that went on in the mainstream schools.

Most of the students were under the age of 10, although one boy, Warren, was 14 years old. He was sitting alone in a corner on his phone while the other kids at the table were doing work. I decided to spend my time talking to Warren so I introduced myself and tried to get him to tell me about the work he did at his mainstream school. I spent about an hour and a half working with him and he went into some detail about his school work on forces in physics. I got him to draw a diagram of how force interacts with materials. He was engaged in the conversation and this first experience of teaching in Saturday school highlighted for me one of the key strengths but also one of the major weaknesses of the programme.

Our long conversation illustrated how relationships can be developed in these small schools that would be far more difficult to establish in a mainstream school setting. I was able to sit down and chat with Warren about various issues and use this as a way to discuss school work. For example, I started the conversation by asking him what he was looking at on his phone and then turned the conversation to the science that makes it work. This eventually led into the conversation about the work he was doing in physics. A one-to-one discussion of this kind would be difficult in a mainstream school, yet the building of relationships is important in helping students to be committed to institutions (Klem and Connell, 2004). However, I cannot be sure that our conversation benefited Warren as it might have suffered from a lack of structure in terms of the work provided for him to do. He may have been better served by a more traditional pedagogy, with set work and assistance. I told him to bring some work for next week that we could discuss, in the hope that his time at the school could be more productive. I was also aware that our conversation, however beneficial, was possible only because the small number of students allowed me to spend so much time with him. Clearly, Saturday schools will have a major effect on schooling only if large numbers attend them, but this would distil the possibility of one-to-one support.

After we left, my sister and I discussed the school's need for more structured activity. That was the overriding impression from our first day there. We talked about the possibility of separating the children according to age and trying some focused activities. We also thought that it may be useful to have a teaching rota so that not everyone had to work the full four hours each Saturday. Even without spending a full day at the school, we could see that volunteering every week would be difficult for people.

13 December
Only one of the teachers from last week, Kamili, was present, plus Luke, a helper from the Uhuru Organization. Again, eleven students were in attendance throughout the day.

I started off by helping a couple of 7 year olds, Shakayna and Mark, with English. They were working through the pages of a mainstream textbook. I also spent some time helping Tobias, aged 5, with mathematics. Some of the morning I spent with Vusi, an intelligent 11 year old who needed more work to do because he found what was asked of him unchallenging and he was soon bored. This part of the day seemed a lot more structured than the previous week. There were three tables and children of different ages sat doing different sets of work. What was clear from my earliest experiences of Saturday school was the strong focus on basic skills and work that would be found in mainstream schools. In this project, which is strongly self-help and run by an organization concerned with African culture, the idea of succeeding in mainstream schools was paramount. The whole morning was dedicated to standard curriculum work.

My sister and I had a good interaction with Makeda, an 11-year-old girl. We asked her to explain the planets in the solar system and she took pride in reciting their names and talking about the differences between them that she had learnt about at school. As with Warren the previous week, we were able to interact and begin to build a relationship with Makeda.

After lunch we all sat in one group and Kamili taught the class and led a discussion about Kwanzaa, the Pan-African celebration held the day after Christmas. Everyone sat in a circle as she took them through the principles of Kwanzaa: unity, self-determination, collective responsibility, cooperative economics, purpose, creativity, and faith. The colours of Kwanzaa are the Pan-African colours of Red, to represent the bloodshed throughout our history; Black, for the colour of the people; and Green, for the land of Africa. Some of the older children knew what the colours represent, perhaps unsurprising as the Red, Black, and Green flag is a vivid symbol of Pan-Africanism popularized by Marcus Garvey. The students spoke about seeing the colours before at home or at events. The ceremony is all about Black people in the West acknowledging and embracing their Africaness, and Kamili spent a lot of time emphasizing this with the class.

Not all students embraced the message of Africaness at first. When Kamili went around the circle asking people if they were African, more than one replied, 'No, I'm Jamaican' and Labraya answered, 'No, I'm from the Cotswolds'. Kamili strove to link all the people in the room to Africa by briefly going over the history of enslavement and explaining Blackness. Some of the younger ones had not heard about enslavement and they seemed genuinely confused by the idea. Though a delicate subject, enslavement should surely form part of the basic education for all Black children. This is where Saturday schools can have a very different impact from mainstream schooling, to some degree offsetting the Eurocentric curriculum of mainstream schools (Dove, 1993).

Eventually, all of the students appeared to get the message and to learn something. Most of the students were attentive and interested in what Kamili told them, though some of the younger ones misbehaved. There were definitely discipline issues with Tobias, a 5-year-old boy, who paid no attention, swinging his legs about and making a lot of noise. Kamili did her best to keep him in line, raising her voice and explaining to him why his behaviour was wrong.

One of the distinct advantages of Saturday schools is the relationships that can exist between student and teacher. This was highlighted that day by the personal stories and experiences Kamili brought into the lesson. When talking about the concept of pride in Blackness and self-determination, she recounted how they had helped her to succeed in school and stay on the right path. She was heartfelt and honest, and this appeared to strike a chord with the students. Hill Collins (2000: 265) talks about the 'ethic of personal accountability' when outlining her Black feminist epistemology, arguing that the conviction and sincerity of the speaker determines who is trusted. I could see this concept at work as Kamili explained the principles of Kwanzaa from her own experiences. I too could use my experience when I spoke about being determined to read *The Autobiography of Malcolm X* when very young. Engaging ourselves in personal discussion allowed the students to talk to us about their experiences. Such conversations were important in building the special relationships at the heart of the programme.

After the talk and discussion, students had to answer questions about Kwanzaa and colour in a picture. This activity went well and helped the children to remember the information while practising their writing skills. Even with the African-centred teaching we strove to get the students to use the skills they needed to succeed in mainstream schools and life in general. The students were engaged in the task and when they finished we listened to a Kwanzaa song. A 4-year-old girl, Sharama, enjoyed it so much she didn't want to leave and had a tantrum when her mom collected her.

17 January
Ten children attended the first session after Christmas. In the morning we went through school work and worksheets from textbooks.

Kamili was on her own when I got there. The other people we'd met on the first day seemed to have left. Kamili explained that John would not be coming back. She was happy about this as they had not got along. Relationships between the members of staff in voluntary projects such as the Lumumba Saturday School are just as important as their relationships with the students. Unlike in mainstream schools, people are not being paid to do a job, so if there are personal difficulties between staff, people may well decide to leave.

24 January
There were eight students at the school when I arrived. We again went through some standard worksheets with the different age groups, trying to get them to focus on learning the basics. I helped students get to grips with numbers and taught some of the younger ones to form letters. This provided the opportunity for one-on-one time and attention, and allowed them to practise and reinforce what they were doing in mainstream schools.

In the afternoon Kemi, a parent, came and gave a talk about Marcus Garvey. We sat all the students in a circle while she gave an account of Garvey's life, also asking the students a lot of questions such as, 'Do you know about slavery?', 'Do you know where your parents are from?' Interestingly, all of the children were aware of their Caribbean descent. Most had family in Jamaica. They were keen to learn, very attentive, and all eager to answer the questions. The question of the students' heritage provoked great enthusiasm. Kemi stressed the importance for Black people to have pride in their Blackness and not to believe that we cannot do things and cannot achieve if that is what we are told.

After Kemi's session the students tackled a worksheet asking five questions about Marcus Garvey and there was great interaction. Kemi asked them the questions as a group and had the students put their hands up to answer, then they all wrote down the answers. The younger students were on different tables, with the other teachers helping them to spell out words they found difficult. The students had a lot of fun and were eager and engaged, writing their answers, then colouring in the worksheet. A couple of parents arrived early and sat and watched the work, joining in, asking the children questions about their heritage and adding information about Marcus Garvey. This reinforcement by the parents was good to see, and they had a chance to participate in their children's learning.

After lessons ended, Kamili, Kemi, and I talked about doing Black history lessons in the afternoons each week. Kemi said she would prepare some materials and come in and run the lessons. She was training to become a teacher and was excellent with the students. I told Kemi and Kamili about the Black history booklet I had made as an undergraduate and other material I had used for teaching.

31 January

When I arrived I found eight students present. In the morning I helped out with maths and also helped a new girl, Natasha aged 5, with her homework. She had to write out sentences with the correct punctuation on a sheet that allowed too little space for her writing. At first I thought she might fit it all in, but then I was not so sure. The problem was that my attention was taken by Mark, who needed a lot of help with his units, tens, and hundreds, although he did it well in the end. This time only Mark benefited from one-to-one attention. I could not focus on Natasha's work. By the time I eventually got round to making her do her writing on a separate sheet she had to repeat the whole exercise.

The Lumumba Saturday School

Two matters arise from this story. One was that I needed to be firmer with her earlier on. When I thought she might need a new sheet I should just have told her to get one, instead of letting her carry on. One downside to volunteers teaching can be their lack of training. Second, staffing is an issue. Kamili and I were alone in the room and although there were only eight students – a situation that most classroom teachers would relish – they were of differing ages and abilities so each required a lot of individual attention. While it might seem like overkill to have any more adults in the room, it could have helped in this situation.

Over lunch the students were pretty quiet and got on with each other quite well. Afterwards they seemed to have a sugar rush and started running around the classroom. I had to use the age-old technique of counting to ten to get them to sit down and be quiet. Kamili spoke to them firmly about respect and listening and had them all help to clean up the room.

We had the children sit in a circle and I asked them the questions about Marcus Garvey from the week before. Again, they were attentive and remembered quite a lot. I asked them why it was important to learn about Black history and what they knew. It was a lively discussion – they all felt it was important to know about their heritage. Then Kamili came in and gave them some information about Queen Nzinga, as a lead-in to Kemi's talk. She began by going round the circle, asking why the children thought it was important to come to Saturday school and to behave when they were there. They replied, 'we have to have respect', 'need to practise what we do in school', 'we will be ahead of the other kids', and 'if you don't then you won't be able to write'. Some of the older students answered that it was 'important to learn' and that 'we need to behave so we can concentrate on work'. Most responses were about how they could improve their school work and advance in mainstream classrooms. Makeda said, 'we need to improve things work wise and also we learn things that we wouldn't learn in normal schools, like Black history'.

This shows that the students were aware of the Black history element and the importance of it in the Saturday School. I stressed the importance of concentrating on work, practising the skills required to succeed in the mainstream curriculum, and learning about areas seldom discussed in mainstream schools. Kamili stressed the importance of behaviour both in and out of the school because they did not want to become criminals, and they needed to have respect and learn things to be ahead of the other children. She became quite impassioned, drawing on the negative stereotypes of Black people to say that we did not want the children to turn into the image as portrayed in the media. It was clearly important to her, and the students listened intently, again evoking Hill Collins's ideas of the 'ethic of personal accountability' (2000: 265). Our voices are heard when people believe we mean our words. This kind of sincerity is encouraged in the close-knit venue of the Lumumba Saturday School.

Kemi then came in and talked about Queen Nzinga, using notes she had prepared. She explained about colonialism in Africa and talked about enslavement. Queen Nzinga was queen of Angola in the early seventeenth century and fought off the colonial advances of the Portuguese until her death. Kemi tied the story into the self-esteem message that had been strongly delivered for a few weeks – that we can do whatever we set out to achieve and we need not let anyone hold us back. She used Queen Nzinga as a vehicle for this message, though also giving the historical facts. Queen Nzinga achieved against the odds and so can all the students. Kemi talked about achievement and went round the circle asking if the students had any achievements and we clapped as they told us about them. They were really engaged and all eager to speak up.

Afterwards we teachers talked about what to do for the following week, and decided to look at Africa as a continent. I volunteered to print out copies of ancient African pictures to show the students. We agreed to go into the school on the Thursday of half-term and decorate the room and talk about plans for the future of the project.

7 February
At lunchtime I wandered around and chatted with the children while they ate. Labraya, who is 7, had a mobile phone that was bigger than her hand. We discussed why she would need a phone at her age. She said she needed to call people, mostly her mom. I chatted to Kamili about nothing in particular – mobile phones, the old days, and plans for the weekend. Relationships between staff are very important to the functioning of the programme – I was aware that Kamili did not get on with John and he ended up leaving.

In the afternoon Kemi came and spoke about ancient Africa. I had printed off a poster for the students to take home. We sat in a circle while Kemi read some material from the internet about the ancient kingdoms and spoke of Kemet, but not all of the material was well researched or accurate. She talked about the kingdoms that spread across Africa before enslavement and how people dressed, but also about what the Europeans came to take away: people and materials. I told the group about how Ghana had so much gold that they made furniture from it (Jackson, 1970). We believed it important to teach about the origins of ancient Africa because our history tends to be represented only from when enslavement began.

Caleb however focused on the issues of enslavement and tied it to racism in the UK. To him the importance of learning about ancient Africa is 'because we as Black people can't get jobs in Britain'. With our aim of discussing Africa before enslavement, it is ironic that we again talked about the legacy of slavery in order to connect to issues in the present day. It is almost impossible not to talk about enslavement because without it the students, the teachers, and the Saturday School would not exist. Kemi showed the children a map of contemporary Africa to give them an idea of the shape and size of the continent and to turn the discussion back to life in Africa before enslavement.

14 February
There were just four students having lunch when I arrived. Only Chris, who is part of the Uhuru Organization and helps out sometimes, was with them and they were noisy and making a mess. Sharama and Jermaine especially (aged 4 and 5 respectively) were misbehaving and I had to tell them off and calm them down. They were not usually badly behaved, but just seemed restless. One of the problems with the Saturday School is that it is all held in one room with nowhere for the students to go to stretch or get some fresh air.

I missed the morning session but Kamili had them writing about what they did in the snow we'd had the week before. As it was half-term we had playtime in the afternoon. I played Connect4 and read Sharama a book, spending time with her because her mom came late. I found out that she was home schooled and thought this explained some of her behaviour, such as the way she went into her shell when with other children. One of the benefits for her of the Saturday School is the chance to mix with children of her own age.

19 February
I went to the Uhuru building to meet Kemi and Kamili to discuss our plans for school. Kamili was late so Kemi and I had a chat about why the popularity of Saturday school was declining. She felt that the state of the building deterred people from coming in and that if there were better facilities, parents would be more likely to bring their kids to the school. She also complained that people never liked to get involved in the community until something really bad happened. For her it all revolves around crisis: if there is a crisis then there is a meeting but not until then. She gave a local example of the city council threatening to take over certain long-held and long-empty community buildings and explained how people had come out to organize and protest, but when the buildings were safe and vacant no one had anything to say. No one wants to get involved on a day-to-day level and do what is necessary.

When Kamili arrived we discussed what we needed for the school and I offered to get a catalogue so that we could choose a bookcase. Kamili had her say on why she thought numbers were declining. She thought children had such a variety of activities now, such as dance classes. In the past there were far fewer places where parents could leave their children. Now there are numerous options that children may find more inviting than extra schooling on the weekend.

28 February

While we were waiting for a Rastafarian teacher who was coming for the afternoon session we got out a big drum and the few children gathered round. We tried to teach them about the significance of the drum throughout Black history – explaining how the drum was used in Africa to communicate between villages and then later in enslavement to point people to freedom. To be honest, they were more interested in banging on it! Labraya was really good and came out with some complex beats. She is 8 years old and her brother plays the African drums.

The presence of the African drum in the classroom is one of the benefits of the Lumumba's connection to the wider Uhuru Organization, to which the drum belongs. Having such items around allows for spontaneous teaching. In the classroom there is also a huge picture of one of the early community events of the 1970s showing thousands of Black people gathered together. The students asked about the picture and we were able to tell them about the long history of resistance by Black people and reinforce the message of Black pride that is central to everything Uhuru does, including the Saturday School.

A Rastafarian lady, Ifrika, came in to talk about Marcus Garvey, reinforcing what we had discussed a couple of weeks earlier. She had the children sit round a table and asked them what they could remember. Ifrika came from a local project and brought other Rastafarians with her to watch the lesson. They were running a competition for children's artwork on Marcus Garvey.

After Ifrika had told the students more about Garvey, she had them do word searches, which we helped them to fill out, and to colour in a picture of Garvey. In truth, the information was printed from the internet and she did not seem to have a depth of knowledge about him. Saturday schools offer the opportunity to engage with a diverse range of people and community organizations but there is no guarantee of the quality of the sessions provided by visitors. I helped Jermaine with his word search as he, at 4, was the youngest student. I am not sure how much of the Black history lessons the younger ones took in.

At the end of the session Kamili, Kemi, and I stayed behind to decide what to do with the £250 I had donated to the school for participating in the research. We made a list of things including books, a bookcase, pens, and paper. They also wanted to organize a trip to either the Slavery Museum in Liverpool or the Empire Museum in Bristol. I agreed to teach about Nanny and enslavement the following week. The topic of enslavement kept arising, but it was not clear whether all of the children understood what it meant.

7 March
After lunch it was my turn to teach about Nanny of the Maroons and enslavement. I used a map of the world and pictures related to the slave trade such as a gun, ancient African kingdoms, the middle passage, a plantation, sugar, and an English lady sipping tea. My aim was to guide them through the history of enslavement using the map. I had them sit in a circle and asked them questions like, 'Where is Africa?' and 'Where is Jamaica?' I tried to make the session interactive by getting them to point to the places on the map. I took them through the reasons for enslavement and the triangular trade between Europe, Africa, and the Americas. They had little knowledge of the details of enslavement, or how there came to be Black people in the Caribbean and the Americas. I had to explain that because there are lots of Black people there now does not mean it has always been that way. I emphasized how those who were enslaved were not seen as people but as cattle to be bought and sold. The older children were engaged and listened intently. The younger ones were not misbehaving but did get a little bored, so I told them about Nanny and her exciting story of being sold into enslavement from Ghana and escaping in Jamaica to lead the Windward Maroons in their fight against the British.

Kemi and Kamili were also in the circle, adding to the story and asking questions of the students. The collaborative nature of the lessons is useful, allowing us to reinforce and build on what the others were teaching. Whether the detailed message of the slave trade got home to the students is doubtful. Kamili asked Caleb what happened during enslavement and his answer was, 'White people used to whip us'. Caleb is only 8 and what stuck with him was the violence of Whites. It is tempting to steer away from the teaching of enslavement because it can be so divisive. After *Roots* was first shown on British television there were clashes between Black and White students in the schools (Warsama, 2007). We nonetheless felt it essential for students to know about this central part of their history. It may well cause ill feeling towards Whites, but the truth remains, as Caleb put it, that 'White people used to whip us'.

After the lesson we had the children complete questions on a worksheet about where Nanny was born and died, what tribe she was from, and so on. We wanted the children to remember the key points: that she was an escaped enslaved African who fought for freedom and organized the Maroons. As always, the Black pride message was key, so it was important that after explaining enslavement we told the story of Nanny, who broke free from her shackles and fought off the British. Even in dreadful times there are redemptive stories.

When I told the parents what we had done in the class I found that some had never heard of Nanny. They all appreciated the Black history element of Saturday school because their children got to learn things about themselves they would not do in mainstream schools. I showed Natasha's mom the map and tried to explain what we were teaching. Her 5-year-old daughter remembered quite a lot about enslavement and Nanny, which she explained to her mother.

The older students remembered most of the information and answered the questions easily. We had to work on the younger students, though; we should have produced different worksheets to suit each age group. It is unrealistic to expect children aged between 4 and 12 to have the same lessons and activities. Every week when we did a Black history lesson we gave them a poster to take home (from the Black history booklet I produced) with information about the figure we learnt about. We wanted them to refer back to the posters when they were older and could understand more. Teaching Black history is not only important for the children – we aimed for the parents to be able to learn from the posters, too. The parents told us that they found the information useful and reinforced it with their children.

Labraya's grandmother was surprised there were not more children at the Saturday School and said there were many more in the school's heyday. A few parents have commented on the decline in its popularity. There were routinely fewer than ten students at the time of the study, yet records indicate as many as 100 had enrolled in the past, with 50 attending regularly. This decline in attendance does raise the question of the relevance of Saturday school today, though all the parents who brought their children were very positive about the programme and surprised that more people did not come. Sharama's mom especially liked the Black history side of the Saturday School. She was passionate about the need to learn about our history so that the children could have 'pride in being Black'.

The Lumumba Saturday School

21 March

My sister stopped coming, although she had been so enthusiastic about volunteering in the Saturday School at first, talking about lots of different ideas for what we could do to make the programme work better. I asked her why she no longer came and she said it was the time commitment that was the biggest obstacle: 'I work full time, five days a week, so giving up my whole Saturday is a lot to ask', she said. This is a major problem in maintaining the movement. It can be difficult to find volunteers who will give up their free time when they also work full time. When we first became involved in the Saturday School my sister suggested that we set up a rota, where people work either the morning or the afternoon, or perhaps on alternate weeks. Menelik had also mentioned starting a rota, but the problem was finding enough volunteers to enable the rota system to function.

I arrived late but apparently so did Kamili, who said she'd arrived at around 10:45. Kemi found parents waiting outside with the children and then had to start the class and give them work to do. This is a major problem: Kamili has to be there early every week and has little help. It comes back to getting more people on board in order to lessen the strain on the volunteers. Having more people on a rota would make it easier to get people involved because we would not be asking them to give up four hours of every weekend.

Kamili was understandably tired and got the children to check each other's work. This helps to foster peer mentoring and develop relationships and a feeling of responsibility. It also helps to firm up the knowledge of those who are giving the help, as they have to explain what they know.

Kamili and Kemi gathered the students in a circle and told them it was important to respect Saturday school and to listen to us in the same way they listen to their parents and school teachers. Sometimes it must be difficult for the students to spend most of their Saturday doing more learning and not get restless, and because the Saturday School is more informal than mainstream school some of the younger children get carried away. However, Kamili is a disciplinarian at times. When she does tell them off, they definitely listen.

After lunch Kemi had planned to talk about Mary Seacole. Although she had printed off some material, she was in no mood to do the lesson, and neither was Kamili, so I took it. One needs to be adaptable and prepared for eventualities. With the voluntary nature of the staff, there are times when you have to fill in.

I got the children to form a circle and again brought out the map that is so useful when teaching Black history, because our history is connected to many continents. I placed the map in the middle of the circle so that all of the students could see it and be involved in pointing out different places.

However, a couple of the children got so enthusiastic about using the map that they could not sit in their chairs. Before we had even started the session I had to threaten that they would not go to the park if they were not quiet. It sort of worked, but I had to repeat this threat throughout the class.

Before we started I went round asking if they liked the Black history lessons. Akeela, who was the oldest at 12, said she liked them because 'they never taught us anything about our history in schools' (a recurring theme). I asked if they had heard of Mary Seacole, a Black nurse for the British troops in the Crimean War. Some of them had and brought up Florence Nightingale (there are reports that Florence Nightingale might have been Creole, according to one of the parents). Kemi chimed in with how Mary Seacole came before Florence Nightingale, but that she was not as popular because she was not White. The children asked if Mary Seacole was better than Nightingale. This is one of the problems when we start to get into 'Negritude', 'the taking pride in Black people who did things before White people', as my father describes it. We start to judge ourselves by the merits of White people. So the focus is not on Seacole's accomplishments and their relevance, but, instead, on whether she is better than the White person. Whatever the limits of Negritude, the students found a kind of comfort in the superiority of Seacole, even though she was held back because she was Black. Makeda vowed to 'never let that happen' to her.

The conversation turned to enslavement, as it always seemed to. Caleb said something about how we used to get beaten during enslavement (he always talked about the violence of slavery). Julian asked why people never 'killed them [White people] in their sleep' instead of being slaves. I gave a not particularly good answer about how sometimes they did, that there were numerous rebellions and in some of them the primary goal was to achieve freedom by killing the White slaveholders, for example, as Nat Turner did in America. I also tried to stress the power the slaveholders had over the enslaved: the gun had enabled the capture and enslavement of Africans in the first place and became the extreme punishment for any enslaved African who rebelled. In America they were outnumbered by the White population, so there was no hope of a revolution, as in Haiti where independence became possible. I mentioned Toussaint and Nanny, who each fought and secured victories in differing degrees against the slaveholders. We need more resources on rebellions during enslavement. We cannot tell the story of enslavement as if the Africans had been passive and did not resist. This is a major danger of the slavery narrative. Black pride is essential, as the teachings in the Lumumba School have made clear, and we should remember that there is much to be proud of in our history of enslavement. At no point did our ancestors submit willingly or give up their dreams of freedom.

28 March
When I arrived the students were studying English. I helped Tobias and Jermaine with their work, going through the letters of the alphabet. Four-year-old Jermaine struggled to get through it. He had yet to start school so we were helping prepare him for the next year. He got quite frustrated but managed to finish it all. When he was done I gave him a high-five and this cheered him up. An older student, Matthew, joined in and gave him a high-five too. It was a nice touch and Jermaine was proud of his work. Separating out the older from the younger kids in mainstream schools means that something is lost. Building relationships across age groups can have a positive effect on the performance of all children (Klem and Connell, 2004). Also, the comparative informality of Saturday school allowed for spontaneous acts such as these. At times there was a strong supportive atmosphere in the classroom, and everyone helped everyone else to succeed.

In the afternoon we talked about Malcolm X. We had settled into a routine with the Black history lessons, which the kids expected. We had them in a circle, then talked with them about a person or place and had them ask and answer questions as we went along. They seemed to look forward to it – well, the older ones did. Kemi could not make the session but had printed out some information from the Black history booklet I created for Kamili. Kamili first recapped things we'd learnt the week before about Mary Seacole and some of the students remembered a lot. Vusi and Makeda even remembered the name of the Crimean War. Kamili read out the information on Malcolm X and as she went through it she asked the children questions about what she was reading. For example, the text says he was a Black nationalist and we had to explain that. It was not easy to find the right words to explain the concept to children aged from 4 to 12. I tried my best, but did not do a good job, which was frustrating as I regularly gave talks about Malcolm's work to university students.

Kamili did not seem too informed about Malcolm, claiming that he rejected Islam before he died. I part clarified what she said, but did not want to say outright that she was wrong and undermine her. Better research was sometimes needed to make sure we had all the information we would need.

We went round and asked the children one thing they had learnt about Malcolm X. Tamika knew the year he was born and almost remembered the year his dad was killed. She had clearly been paying attention to the session. The younger ones were a bit nonplussed. All Tobias could offer was that 'he was a man' and Labraya remembered that he was Black. Mark came out with 'he's bad' and when asked why he thought this, he replied, 'because he was a criminal'. Kamili tried to explain about looking at the positives, asking, 'what did he do after he left prison?' None of the students was really able to answer this, for the reason that we never actually told them. The booklet definitely needs to be updated to reflect what he did, other than preach about the Nation of Islam, and to stress why Malcolm is so important.

This session evoked a discussion about prisons, what happens in them, and why they are bad. Students were afraid of not being free and the older boys did not want to go to prison because, as Julian put it, they 'don't want to be raped'. Kamili went round the circle and got them to answer 'what are prisons for?' Most of the kids said something like 'naughty people', while Julian came out with 'Black people', again showing the awareness children have from a young age of negative stereotypes. The answer Kemi gave was 'to dehumanize you' and she explained how prisons broke down the individual. Julian talked about visiting prison when he was younger and wanting to see Mandela's cell. Kamili made it clear that none of the kids was going to end up in prison. She said, 'We're too good for that, we don't want you ending up in prison.' I can see the motivation behind the comments: to give children pride in themselves and get them to aim high, but perhaps the expectations that we have of Black young people are too low. As we saw in Chapter 5, a theme from the interviews was the fear that Black young people were being lured into street life. Kamili's impassioned talk about staying out of prison ties into that narrative. Were any of the children thinking about prison as a possible destination? Should we, however implicitly, be sending the message that not finding yourself in prison is an achievement in itself?

We had the children answer questions about the topic while Jermaine and Tobias drew a picture of Malcolm X because they were so young. Tobias got excited about drawing the picture and did a pretty good one.

I spoke to Tamika's mom and asked if she thought her daughter was enjoying the Saturday School. She was absolutely clear: 'It doesn't matter, they don't teach Black history in school.' She was adamant that the history aspect was extremely important and the reason she had enrolled her daughter in the programme. I also told Tobias's mom he was doing a lot better. She was surprised and said she thought I was going to tell her he was banned for three weeks. She was obviously happy about the progress he had made.

4 April
The only students at the Lumumba School when I arrived came with Kemi (Caleb and some children I had never met) and Tobias and Mark, who are

brothers. It was school holiday time and when schools are closed parents tend to think that Saturday school is too, so do not always bring their children in. This suggests the parents see a connection between mainstream and supplementary school.

Kamili commented that some of the students had been missing for a while, including Vusi and Sharama. It had happened a lot in the past that a child did not attend regularly or dropped out without notice. Ultimately, you cannot force people to attend, but it does make it difficult to plan for the long term. The flexibility is an essential part of the benefit of Saturday schools for parents, but at the same time poses difficulties for the staff.

While in the Lumumba School I came across a board game called 'Identity', a Black heritage game that helps children learn about their history by going round a board and answering questions about different Black heroes. I took the game away for a week because I wanted to see if I could work it out before playing it with the students. I never did work it out, it was so complicated. More importantly, there were no figures in the game that predated enslavement. It was an American game, so it featured African Americans who had achieved in some field such as business or science, along traditional Negritudinal lines, plus key figures such as Malcolm X, Martin Luther King, and Booker T. Washington. The message from this game was clear: 'Your history starts with slavery and is limited to national borders.' The Black history message in the game is utilized only as a vehicle to boost pride and promote self-uplift in Black youth.

The Black history or, as Menelik would say, 'African history', lessons in the Lumumba School were not simply about messages of pride and the psychological benefits, though this is important. The real power of the African link is that it ties us to the Diaspora of Black people worldwide. We learn about our roots not just for self-fulfilment but to connect us to the other branches of the tree. This is one of the key features of Black radical politics and illustrates Menelik's distinction between 'Black' and 'African' history. Pan-Africanism takes a different view, namely that we cannot be disconnected from other Black peoples. So the African history taught in spaces such as the Lumumba School brings in figures from America, the Caribbean, Africa, and pre-enslaved societies. This history is essential to connect us to Africa and therefore the Diaspora, not solely because of pride but to connect us to an international politics where we work for the freedom of all Black people no matter where we reside. It is this fundamental principle that underlies the teaching of history in the Lumumba School: there can be no freedom for Black people anywhere unless there is freedom for Black people everywhere, and the key to this is Africa.

16 May

This was the first time I had attended the Saturday School in a few weeks, for various reasons. When I arrived only Kemi and Chris were there with the students. Kamili had said she would miss the previous week, but I was not sure where she was this week. Attendance of staff can fluctuate as much as that of the students, as my non-attendance demonstrated. When I arrived, Kemi was just getting out a book about animals they had gone through the previous week and was preparing an activity for the afternoon in which the students were to make some pretty animals out of card.

I was thrown in at the deep end, teaching a class to the seven students present. They were sitting in a semicircle around a whiteboard with a chart on it displaying information on animals they had read about in a book with Chris the week before. I had not seen the book and had no idea what was going on so I just had to feel my way through the lesson. The children had told me that they knew how to spell the names of all of the animals they had learnt about. I had the copy of the book so went through it, starting with an elephant. I got them first to spell it and then to tell me what it ate and where it lived. I had to ad lib information about herbivores, carnivores, and omnivores, and made sure I used examples for each. Every time I gave them a new word I got them to spell it collectively, then repeat it.

The relationships I had built with the pupils came into play. They were comfortable to ad lib their way through the lesson with me. Had they not known me, I imagine that this would have been disastrous. I made sure I added quite a bit of information and they were all engaged, asking and answering questions about animals and spelling. It helped that I came across as knowledgeable.

However well the class went, though, we would definitely have benefited from having some sort of lesson plan in place beforehand that made clear who was running the session. In general, I found the Lumumba Saturday School quite disorganized. Weekly meetings to discuss who is doing what so they can draw up lesson plans had been suggested but never materialized. The benefit of official programmes delivered by qualified teachers is that they are experienced at doing preparation and if they are getting paid for their time they have the incentive to do the extra work involved. Our less structured approach could work and I would say the students did learn, but we could have organized the time to maximize what the students got out of the programme.

In the afternoon activity the students stuck tissue paper on pictures of animals. I was not sure of the educational value of this but the students seemed to enjoy doing it. There was no Black history element this week as we were focusing on the animals. The following week we were taking them to the nature centre to look at some animals, using the money I had donated to the school for participating in the research.

It was good to see the diverse nature of the topics taught at the Lumumba School. It was not simply the basics of maths and English plus Black history. I was excited to see that there was a field trip to put the learning of this week into use.

Kemi had instituted the recitation of the *African Pledge* for the students to officially open and close the Saturday School. The idea is based on the pledge of allegiance to the flag that American students make in school. When I came in I caught the end of it, then witnessed it in full at the end of the day. The pledge goes as follows:

> We are an Afrikan People!!
> We will remember the humanity, glory, and suffering of our ancestors.
> We will honour the struggles of our elders.
> We will strive to bring new values and new life to our people.
> We will have peace and harmony among us.
> We will be loving, sharing, and creative.
> We will work, study, and listen so we may learn, learn so we may teach.
> We will cultivate self-reliance.
> We will struggle to resurrect and unify our homeland.
> We will raise many children for our nation.
> We will have discipline, patience, devotion, and courage.
> We will live as models to provide new directions for our people.
> We will be free and self-determining.
> We are an Afrikan people,
> And we will win (x3).

Commitment to Africaness stands out in the pledge and reinforces the importance of the Diaspora. As Africans we have certain responsibilities to one another and are tied together by our common descent. The pledge works along the lines of self-belief and commitment to Diaspora, themes that have been evident throughout my time at the Saturday School. It is also very hopeful and positive, as it outlines what 'we will' achieve. It ends with the words 'we will win' because the Black radical position is always the optimistic one. The pledge is from America but is being used in the British context because the issues transcend national boundaries and go to the heart of the politics of Diaspora. Kemi is very keen on the political dimension to the teaching. A few of the parents were there for the pledge and all spoke positively about bringing it into the school. One of the main reasons they bring their children to the Lumumba School is for the Black history and connection to Africa.

13 June
An outbreak of flu had closed the local schools and the Lumumba School for a couple of weeks. When I arrived this week only three students were present: Akeela, Labraya, and Sharama. Akeela was working on magnets, so I looked at her work and took her through some of the questions. She seemed to know the information pretty well, and was confident when I asked her questions that were not on her worksheet. Working with students one to one is a good way for them to learn and also to build relationships with their teachers.

While the students were eating lunch, a visitor, Mable, came in from Uganda. She had just moved to the UK and had found the Uhuru Organization on the city council's volunteer website. It surprised us all that the organization was on the website, given the radical nature of Uhuru and the antagonistic history between them and the council. It shows the thawing of relations with local government, also reflected in the nominal funding they gave to the school.

Mable was interested in volunteering at the Saturday School. I did not get too excited at the prospect of another teacher because we had seen people before who showed interest and then were never seen again. We introduced her to the students and asked them if they knew where Uganda was. The children's faces were mostly blank but Akeela did say that it was in Africa. When Mable asked what we taught them, Kamili told her maths, English, and science, but made no mention of Black history. I was surprised because Kamili has never been reticent about Black history lessons and seemed to enjoy leading them. It may just have been a meaningless slip, or she may simply have prioritized the subjects we do in the morning sessions.

After lunch we took the students out to the park. It was good to get them some fresh air, which we had planned to do once the weather improved. At the park, Kamili recalled a time she had seen loads of Black people on a roundabout in the park. It was an important part of her growing up, being with friends and specifically being around other Black children. Some of the students at the Lumumba School come from the other side of the city and do not live in an area with a significant Black population. Matthew and Julian's dad spoke about the need for them to come to the school to get the 'Blackness side of things', because they lived across the city.

Kamili mentioned that there might be a summer school, but was unsure about the funding, which they had so far not received from the council. It was apt that the issue of funding would arise again in the last session. The summer school did not run that year because it received no money from the state: lack of funds was, as ever, a problem that stalks the history of Black supplementary education.

Chapter 8
Lessons from the Lumumba

The experiences detailed in the previous chapter offer insights into the issues facing the Black supplementary school movement. This chapter discusses the lessons learnt from the Lumumba School and how these relate to the Black supplementary school movement in general. It goes on to outline some of the challenges for the future of Black supplementary schools, drawing on my experiences in the Lumumba School.

Successes of the programme

Relationships
Relationships were key to how the Lumumba School functioned. Strong relationships were possible in part because of the small student numbers and even smaller number of staff, allowing close contact and enabling rapport with the students. We engaged with the students and talked about issues other than the work. We took them on trips and often spoke informally with their families. It was clear who was in charge in the classroom, but there was also room for the students to relax and enjoy the experience with their teachers. This is far from the practice of all Black supplementary schools; in more official programmes, professional teachers are often used and they sometimes prefer to maintain similar relationships to those in mainstream classrooms.

In the Saturday school run by Jason, interviewed in Part One, one teacher took a more extreme disciplinarian approach than would be found in the strictest of mainstream schools. This teacher believed that schools needed to return to the old-school values they used to have in Jamaica, with total respect shown to the teacher. His preferred method of teaching was to rule the classroom with an iron fist. I have found that this is not uncommon within the Black community. There is much pining for the 'good old days' of discipline in schools. A fine example of this arose when a local radio presenter had the chance to interview David Cameron in 2008. Instead of questioning him about his regressive plans for the Black community, the presenter ranted on about the problems of the lack of respect among Black youth and appealed to the Conservative to bring back the cane if he ever got into office. The presenter argued:

> Kids ... have no respect for any authority at all starting with the schools, with no respect for their teachers, they've no respect for their parents and they've no respect for ... the police ... it's because they've got no fear. I mean the cane used to instil fear in children.

This approach is the antithesis of the relationships that were created in the Lumumba School and rests on a wholly different set of beliefs about the Black community. If we take the position that lack of discipline is the problem we end up blaming ourselves for the problems in the community. The argument is that if Black youth had the correct level of respect beaten into them at school or in the home, they would not be in the position they are in and all would be well. At the Lumumba School no one saw the students as deviants who needed to be controlled.

Partly because Kamili and I were under 26, while Kemi was a parent, we set out to engage the students. There were times when stricter discipline was called for and when voices were raised and children reminded that the teachers were in control, even though we were not in a mainstream classroom. However, we attempted a strongly interactive teaching method that allowed students to engage with the learning process. We encouraged discussions and students felt comfortable talking about issues of racism and the experiences they had in school. I regard this as one of the key successes of the Lumumba School. The students liked coming to the programme – important for anything held on a Saturday – and they liked seeing the teachers. However, one issue that arises is discipline.

Discipline

Central to critical pedagogy is a flattening-out of the authority in the student–teacher relationship (Freire, 1972). Creating a dialectic relationship is key in forming a student–teacher, teacher–student compact. A Freirean model serves as the foundation for much critical pedagogy, but, significantly, this model is based on his work with teaching adults, so the challenges are different from those concerning children. The issue of age is crucial. In adult education the students may be of a similar age to the teacher, or older. This greatly facilitates breaking down the traditional relationship because of social codes. The figure of the harsh disciplinarian ruling with the cane is not evoked; it would be unacceptable to treat your social equal in such a way. Freire's (*ibid.*) model of the dialectical approach is about challenging the traditional figure of the teacher holding absolute knowledge and bestowing information on the students. However, discipline becomes an issue when working with young people in a collaborative way. Maintaining control of the classroom is vital.

Throughout my time at the Lumumba School the need for strong discipline was constantly apparent. Certain students were challenging, testing the boundaries of acceptability in the classroom. Tobias, the most difficult, was only 5 years old. He had just started mainstream school and was clearly unused to the boundaries in the classroom. There was no prospect of making him a student–teacher in a dialectical sense because of problems with discipline, as well as his age. We gave the students a good deal of leeway and while this allowed them greater freedom of expression, it also led them to become excited and unruly at times. For example, group discussions would sometimes end up with all the students wanting to say something at the same time, relevant or not, and we would have to stop the session to reiterate the rules about respecting everyone's opinion. After we played games with them at lunchtime, the students would be reluctant to recognize our authority and would challenge us by not complying with our requests. When this happened we had to reinforce our position as in authority by stopping the games, reprimanding the children, and sometimes punishing them with work that was less fun than we had planned.

When working with children the issue of discipline is central to a well-functioning teaching environment. Some teachers put discipline at the centre of their relationship with students, but a strict disciplinarian approach does not fit with a critical pedagogical stance on teaching. The teacher–student relationship is defined by whether the teachers are attempting to bestow knowledge on the children, or dialectically construct it with them.

Political education

It is possible to have a disciplinarian teacher in a supplementary school whose lessons seek to instil Black radical theory in the students and to fill the empty receptacles of their minds with the 'correct' radical ideology. However, the goal of a radical approach should be political education, not indoctrination. The production and uncritical assimilation of elite knowledge is one way in which racism is unthinkingly reproduced by society. Black radical approaches to education should not be similarly dogmatic and repressive. They should instead seek to produce students and teachers who are critical and political. Our role should be to involve students in a critique of society that develops a commitment to transform the conditions they face. Fostering a communicative relationship with the students at the Lumumba School was therefore central to a progressive Black supplementary education.

However, critical approaches to pedagogy are weakened by concerns not to indoctrinate students. It is possible to become too depoliticized. Unwittingly we end up supporting the status quo if we do not advocate an alternative agenda and simply aim to 'assist social-justice-oriented individuals in organizing to actively do something', with no definition (Milner, 2008: 339). We must avoid dogma, but if we fail to engage with our own position we collude in the dogma of silence. Change requires politics, and politics requires ideology. Those who believe in radical change must endorse a radical ideology. We should avoid dogmatic preaching in our pursuit of a Black education and not shy away from our commitment to a dialectic approach to learning. Our goal as Black radical educators should be to produce students who can critique society and the political position from which we present our education. Black education must be overtly both Black and radical in its standpoint, but must also allow for the challenge and critique of the student. We must believe that our position is correct and that our students will endorse it. What is taught is equally critical, and here I point to another success of the Lumumba Saturday School: its curriculum.

Curriculum

One of the main reasons parents said they brought their children to the Lumumba School was so they could learn about Black history and culture. Admittedly this expectation was due largely to the reputation of the school and not its practice. When I began teaching at the school, little Black history was taught. However, the issue of Black history is about more than the curriculum. On entering the Lumumba School one is struck by the messages of Blackness in the posters on the walls, ranging from African kingdoms to local events, and the collection of books. Blackness and Black history permeate the school whatever the lesson.

Within the Black supplementary school movement Black history has often been seen as an alternative to mainstream academic subjects. In light of the reputation of the Uhuru Organization it might be expected that Black history would be prioritized over all else. Indeed, when interviewed Errol told me that 'you can't get a job by learning about Africa'. His assumption that the school taught only Black history was quite mistaken. The emphasis lay on basic skills and on succeeding in mainstream school. That we taught maths, English, and science was not in question. The idea was to teach the students as much as possible about as many topics as we could, but never to lose sight of the importance of Black history.

Studying Blackness and mainstream work are not mutually exclusive. This is a hard argument to have with proponents of the official supplementary schools, whom I have found are quick to denounce the study of Black history and political and critical education. These sentiments are captured in the words of Stone (1981: 246) when she writes, 'left-wing teachers have done more harm to Black children'. Her contention is that students need to get qualifications to succeed so everything should be driven by this principle. Her anti-Black studies approach misses two key factors. First, that though the emphasis in some self-help projects (though the Lumumba School cannot stand as evidence for all) is not on school grades, this does not mean that there is no commitment to developing the skills the students need to succeed. When a supplementary school is committed to a 'holistic' approach to education, as Menelik describes, it is not necessary to spell out that this includes teaching such skills. Second, the notion of the competing sides of mainstream and self-help is based on an outdated concept that self-help programmes are in conflict with the state.

Supporting the schools

The history of the Lumumba School is a testament to the fractious relationship between Black supplementary schools and the state when the movement began. Some of the views about the early supplementary schools expressed by Menelik reflect the opposition and conflict with mainstream schooling. In its early days the school used to teach the children and parents radical material such as Marxist-Leninism, which upset some mainstream school teachers. However, this approach was oppositional rather than a radical move to overthrow the mainstream school system, and the anti-school stance that existed in the past is a myth today.

Although there had been conflict with local councils, in the past, with radical teachings extolling seizure of the state, supplementary schools had nonetheless been orientated around helping students succeed in mainstream education. Learning to read, write, and do maths and science are helpful not only for students to get good grades but also for the revolution. The radical discourse on mainstream education, as I have witnessed it, is that the schools are inherently corrupt but have to be used as a tool to succeed. As Jason said in an interview, 'we have to equip the students to survive the schools'. So students were encouraged to get through the schools, not to overturn them.

Such conflict with the state has all but disappeared today. Supplementary education has been accommodated into local educational policy by the provision of funds and, increasingly, quality standards. Even the more radical self-help projects such as the Lumumba School have received some state funds. There are no longer pitched battles with heads of local councils. Although the mainstream certainly came in for criticism, at the Lumumba School effort was made to encourage students in their maintained schools. To get through school the students need something they cannot get from the mainstream (Chevannes and Reeves, 1989).

The all-Black atmosphere, where students can talk openly about racism and their problems in school, helps to keep the students on track. Without the forum the Saturday School provides it is unlikely that the students would have been able to raise issues such as those that came up during the Black history sessions. Several times one or other student would make reference to the racism they were dealing with. Caleb spoke about being one of the only Black kids in his year and how this made him feel he had to fight the other boys when they called him racist names. We were able to discuss as a group why he felt like this and explore better ways for him to deal with his frustration. We used the Black history curriculum to get Caleb to think of heroes with whom he could identify and consider what they would have done in his shoes. Kamili was constantly preaching about the need to do well in school so as to get a good job. Kemi was more radical in her political views and quicker to denounce the system, but she too emphasized the need to do well in school. The mainstream was critiqued on the one hand, and negative experiences there acknowledged, but support and guidance were offered on how to overcome the circumstances and achieve. The unique and central benefit of Black supplementary schools, the Black-led environment, cannot be underestimated.

Black-led environment

As Reeves and Chevannes reported about their Black supplementary school programme, the 'fraternity of colour is an important aspect of the school's success in pupils' eyes' (1983b: 8). It was free of the discrimination that existed in mainstream schools and the students could discuss issues of race and racism. Students in the Lumumba School talked about the classroom as their own space. Caleb declared, 'I like Saturday school because it is ours. We can be ourselves here.' We could address issues and talk about Blackness without having to filter our views because everyone in the classroom was Black. I found this positive particularly because it's important to be careful with the language you use when talking about issues such as enslavement and racism. For instance, if you say to a group of students that Paul Bogle in Jamaica wanted to drive all the Whites into the sea, issues are raised when some of them are White. Talking about the horrors of enslavement can stir resentment between different groups in a class. In an all-Black environment there is a different dynamic – the teacher does not have to fear causing offence. This is not to say that anything goes and that we spend the session 'cursing Whitey'. However, it does allow a level of freedom for discussion and this is important. The topic of enslavement is foundational when understanding issues of Blackness and race in the UK.

Do you remember the days of slavery?

I have used Black in the Diasporic sense, to speak of all those of African ancestry, but there are ethnic differences among Black groups. The area where the research was carried out has seen little migration of people directly from Africa until relatively recently. When we talk about the history of Black people in the city, we mean primarily African Caribbean people. This is true of the Black supplementary school movement too, and certainly true of the Lumumba School and the Uhuru Organization. In one sense this makes the discussion and the learning about enslavement paramount, because we are all descended from enslaved Africans. These really are our stories. My experience of teaching in the Lumumba School demonstrated that one cannot understand Black history without understanding the story of the enslavement of African people. Enslavement is the hub through which everything connects and follows.

What I found, however, was that the students knew very little about enslavement. Admittedly they were young but even the older students had very limited knowledge of their history. My experiences at the school and the accounts of the students indicate that they had not studied enslavement in the mainstream schools. Given its centrality to the foundation of modern Britain, the study of enslavement should be mandatory in mainstream schools. However, to judge from the 'celebrations' of the bicentenary in 2007 of the Abolition of the Slave Trade Act, this is not a topic that we should entrust the mainstream schools to teach. The Black-led space is perhaps the perfect environment for teaching about the history of enslavement even though this does ghettoize the legacy of enslavement to Black people, when it is equally important for everyone in Britain to understand.

However, we need to be careful how we teach about enslavement. It is easy to fall into the trap of portraying Africans as passively accepting the fate forced on them by their White masters. One of our students, Julian, asked us why the Africans did not fight back and 'kill them [Whites] in their sleep'. We must focus on the long history of rebellions to enslavement: the story should be of sadness but also pride. We were not made powerless in the process; our power was stolen from us at the barrel end of a gun, but that did not stop people from fighting to liberate themselves and our people. Nor should we limit Black history to enslavement but should explore precolonial Africa and relate enslavement to today's society. Making connections with the past helps us to understand the present, and the students were quick to link their lessons about enslavement with their awareness of racism.

Caleb in particular always linked our Black history lessons to his feelings of injustice about contemporary society. Although this is essential, we must take care not to stoke students' anger. While the connection with the history of enslavement is fundamental to our role in society today, the nature of discrimination has changed. White people are not the enemy and if we send out the students believing they are, we will make things worse for them in schools, not better. Yet another misconception that I have encountered about the Lumumba School is that the lessons are about hating White people and stirring up anger. In fact, the school discouraged anger or resentment and instead encouraged students to use the lessons positively to take greater pride in themselves. Such is the nature of ethnographic research that the Lumumba School cannot stand as typical of all self-help projects. However, it has one of the longest traditions and most radical reputations of any Black supplementary school. More importantly, the practice we developed in the school demonstrates that we can teach about sensitive subjects honestly and without driving the students to fits of violence and resentment.

The challenges facing Black supplementary schools

Structure

One of the enduring complaints about self-help supplementary school programmes is that they lack formal structure (Stone, 1981). Self-help programmes are organized by a number of agents, from groups of concerned parents to organizations such as Uhuru. Often nobody involved has formal experience of teaching, so there may well be issues around how activities are structured. From the first visit I was surprised about the lack of a discernible structure in the Lumumba School. Because it had run for so long, I expected to find a clear structure in place. Until we instituted the Black history sessions in the afternoons, however, there was no real plan as to what to do with the day. My sister likened it to babysitting because we just seemed to be watching the children much of the time. The person who had run the classes had left a couple of weeks before I arrived, leaving no lesson plans, and it was not clear who was in charge.

Eventually we developed a structure: mainstream work in the morning and Black history in the afternoon, although the work in the morning was still loosely structured, with few lessons. It was more a case of helping the students through either homework or work in textbooks, and sometimes we struggled to find things for them to do. Not knowing what they were studying or what each student should know, I found it difficult to set work for them. The benefits of official programmes run by qualified teachers are obvious in this regard. However, we worked with what we had and got the students involved in picking out work and bringing in their homework. We made efforts to ask them what they needed help with, and we usually managed to find appropriate work for them to do.

The Black history lessons were purposefully run in a way that encouraged student involvement. The students were free to ask questions and the other teachers interjected when they wished. A more formal structure might have inhibited the openness that characterized the sessions. However, some of the lessons, for example, the one about Queen Nzinga, might have been unstructured and the information not entirely accurate, so detailed lesson plans would have helped. Overall, the best was done with the experience, knowledge, and time at our disposal.

My experience of the Lumumba School is not typical of all self-help projects. In fact, the school has a history of strong lesson plans and organization at times in its history. When I helped to clean out a store cupboard at the project I found a bundle of old lesson plans and registers. From talking to parents, some of whom had been to the Lumumba School as children, it became clear that in their day the planning and organization was good. The main determinant of the degree of structure and organization was the people who volunteered to teach. When they had experience of education they brought it to the supplementary school. To overcome a lack of structure requires having a good many people to help out. This raises an issue that limited the Lumumba School: the absence of a staff rota.

The issue is a chicken-and-egg scenario: there can only be a rota when there are enough people, but you can only keep enough volunteers by having a rota. When I first went to the school there were three other teachers, so there appeared to be the opportunity for creating a rota. However, within two weeks the other two teachers had stopped volunteering.

Credit must go to the volunteers; it is they who make supplementary schools work. The Lumumba School could not have functioned without the commitment of Kamili, who came in early every week and left late to make sure that the students had a place to come to learn. She would have welcomed support such as training to create lessons plans and structure the environment.

Coordination

The isolation of Black supplementary schools historically has prevented the development of training schemes for volunteers. My research shows that supplementary schools are disconnected from each other and that it is difficult for parents and potential volunteers to find them. The lack of connections makes catering for the needs of volunteers and students more difficult than if there were a network coordinating the different programmes. While I was at the Lumumba School I saw no contact with any other programmes in the city. We could have collaborated on trips and perhaps even shared volunteers. Supplementary schools are typically set up by concerned members of the community, almost always in isolation of other efforts. Building networks to connect the endeavours could greatly support the work. The development of the National Association of Black Supplementary Schools (NABSS), discussed in Chapter 3, is refreshing in this regard, but it owes its existence to the passion Nia Imara has put into creating a network for the movement. Similar endeavours failed in the past because the individuals behind them were not supported by the movement. Building on the work of NABSS is essential to the future of Black supplementary schools.

Declining attendance

The biggest issue facing Black supplementary schools is the decline in attendance. Student numbers were at their peak from the late 1970s to the early 1990s. As we have seen, the highest number of students coming to the Lumumba School was eleven and often there were only five or six. Menelik told me that in the peak years up to 50 students attended each week, requiring the use of several rooms in the building, and registers from the 1980s confirm these numbers.

As we saw in Chapter 7, Kamili and Kemi advanced reasons for the lack of numbers, including the state of the building and the problems with advertising the school. Although NABSS complained that people do not always know about the supplementary schools in their area, the Lumumba School is one of the longest-running supplementary programmes; it is very well known in the local area and advertises on Black radio stations. The Uhuru Organization is also well known.

Kamili focused on the opportunities available for children at the weekends that were not present in the past. She frequently spoke of students telling her they were at dance class, or doing some other activity that prevented them from attending. This argument makes sense, especially because it has always been problematic getting older students to attend once they can choose not to. While the declining numbers reflect the competing distractions in contemporary society, there are deeper issues affecting Black supplementary schools that need to be examined in light of the reasons why they were first formed.

Black supplementary schools were a reaction to the failure of state schools to provide for Black schoolchildren. Discriminatory practices such as busing Black children from their inner-city schools (see Killian, 1979) in the 1960s led to a consensus that mainstream school provision was failing their children. Stone reported in 1981 that 'West Indian parents and their adolescent children have very little faith in the British school system' (175). The need for supplementary schools was unquestioned during the 1970s and into the 1990s; it was a given that racism was endemic and that Black children were denied the opportunity to learn the basics they needed to progress in school and in the future. This discourse that is critical of the schools has fundamentally changed.

The attention to the issue of Black achievement in schools by the Rampton Report (1981) and Swann Report (1985), alongside continued race relations legislation, has presented an image of the state as actively concerned to make educational provision for all children. Over the years Black achievement has risen significantly in the sense that a much greater proportion of Black children attain the requisite five A*–C grades at GCSE level (Steven, 2007). What has also occurred is a shift in the discourse from blaming the schools, and back to locating the problem in the 'underachievement' of Black students. As we saw in Chapter 4, Reeves and Chevannes (1983a) forewarned against the Black community adopting the language of underachievement, because it was an ideological construction that placed the blame for low achievement in the cultural deprivation of Black communities. In this discourse it is not the racist teacher who is responsible for inequalities in education, but the abnormal Black family and community environment with its dearth of positive male role models. No longer is the ire of the Black community reserved for the schools, but there is a growing cadre of Black opinion makers who endorse and reproduce the ideology of Black underachievement and cultural deprivation (see the discussion of Sewell in Chapter 4).

The effect of rising standards and a shift in discourse has been to undercut the primary argument for the necessity of supplementary schools: i.e. for parents to get their children an education. In the Lumumba School today, parents gave different reasons for taking their children to the programme. They are overwhelmingly motivated by the cultural and Black history aspects of the curriculum even though there has always been 'an overriding concern with the teaching of basic skills' (Stone, 1981: 186). When parents have faith that the basic educational needs of their children will be met by the mainstream schools, we see a decline in the popularity of Black supplementary programmes. Today the parents whose children attend are those who are interested in their children experiencing a Black curriculum. The mass popularity of the movement in the 1970s to early 1990s was based on a critique of schooling that is no longer endorsed by the majority of Black parents.

Yet the rise in standards that has occurred for Black students is illusory (Gillborn, 2008). While achievement for Black students has improved by all measures, so has the achievement of all other ethnic groups. Gillborn argues that the achievement gap has remained relatively consistent over the decades and that the relative position of Black students in the school system is as unequal today as it has ever been. Arguably, then, the primary reason for sending Black children to supplementary schools is as pressing as ever. However, due to state action and shifting discourse the Black community has allowed a central feature of our challenge to educational and social inequality to atrophy. As Bell (1992: 3) observed about inherently racist societies, 'what we designate as "racial progress" [in this case improved achievement at school] is not a solution to that problem. It is a regeneration of the problem in a particularly perverse form.'

Conclusion

My experiences in the Lumumba School pointed to some directions for the future. The strengths of the schools include the relationships between teachers and students and the delivery of support for the mainstream, as well as a Black studies curriculum. Yet a number of challenges for the futures of the supplementary schools were also apparent: the structure and coordination of programmes need developing, and strategies are required to increase attendance. The analysis of my experiences at the Lumumba School offers an understanding of Black supplementary schools to anyone interested in the future development of the movement.

Conclusion
Resisting racism

Black supplementary schools began as a grassroots movement in Black communities to challenge racial inequalities in the British school system. This book has offered an account of the underlying principles and tensions in the movement drawn from three pieces of research and a reading of the literature. The concluding chapter highlights the limitations of the study, points to future research, and draws out the main lessons from the book. The factors highlighted by the study are pulled out below.

Parents' voices
Supplementary schools are embedded within the communities from which they arise. So they rely for their survival on the relationships they build up with parents. However, I have not made a systematic effort to capture the voice of parents.

Though comments from parents were captured in the ethnographic study, there were no formal interviews with the parents. Yet such is the nature of the movement that the majority of those interviewed were or had been the parents of children who attended supplementary schools. Indeed, the supplementary schools featured in the archival project of the New Beacon collective were started by parents in their own homes.

The book focuses on the people who ran supplementary school projects and gives a detailed ethnography of my experiences teaching inside a programme. The aim was to analyse the movement itself and what it is offering, rather than the motivations of parents as consumers or the views and voices of students. The views of the parents featured in the decisions made by those who ran the schools and are essential in determining the future of the movement. For example, Sonia reported that her supplementary school had become more focused on preparation for exams because the fee-paying parents demanded this. However, the parents' role in the supplementary school movement is not simply as consumers who order the service they require.

Parents were discussed in all of the interviews. The general consensus was that the newer generation had a different set of priorities. A number of participants spoke about the individualism of the parents and their reluctance to engage in and support supplementary schools. The concern expressed most often about the future of the movement was the disengagement of parents today. Appeals were made in the interviews for parents to get more involved and carry on the tradition. Efforts were also made to engage parents with the Black history curriculum, as the participants saw this as important knowledge for themselves as well as their children. Black supplementary schooling is not provided only to meet the demand from parents but rather strives to engage and educate parents in the vision of education that is being created in the programmes.

Research into the parental view of the service supplied by Black supplementary schools would be of value. However, the complex relationship of parents to the supplementary schools must be appreciated. The movement is such that it will never be shaped solely by parental demand.

The experiences of the students
The viability of the Black supplementary school movement depends on the continued engagement of the students. A key finding in this study was that retaining older students was particularly difficult. The reasons advanced for this included the availability of alternatives and the lack of desire to spend the weekend learning. The only way to find out why students do not want to attend or why they drop out once they are in secondary school is to ask them.

But the supplementary schools do not cater only to the desires of the students any more than they do to the wants of the parents. Those who run the programmes are clear about the purpose of the education they provide. However, though the subject matter may be determined to some extent by the educational philosophy of the supplementary school, the pedagogy could be more flexible. Often supplementary schools mimic the teaching styles of the mainstream schools, and this could be a deterrent for older students. Future research could examine the innovative forms of pedagogy that have been developed in some programmes and explore whether these could be more widely used to retain older students. The Black supplementary school movement is facing serious pressure for its survival, and it may be necessary to find innovative ways to attract students.

Blackness and a globalized world
A major aspect of my research was to analyse the role of Blackness in the Black supplementary school movement. Blackness, defined in connection with the African Diaspora, has been essential to the movement and forms the basis of the collective endeavour. As detailed in Chapter 2, this contradicts the dominant view of seeing race as a by-product of racism, which is outdated. Such a view must be resisted. It is tied to the idea that society has

been drastically altered by globalization, which reduces the importance of collective groupings around race.

According to the globalization thesis, global capital has dissolved the sovereignty of the nation state and multinational corporations have disempowered the trade unions and created job insecurity (Munck, 2002). In this analysis, the globalized world is hallmarked by fracture and uncertainty, and the old collective forms of action, through nations and the labour movement, are outdated. However, when we conceptualize society in this fractured way, our reaction to injustice also becomes fragmented. Gone is the union of workers against an organized system of business and the nation state, replaced by individual complaints through the human resources departments of individual companies. We act only when our individual human rights are infringed and this leads to single-issue campaigns. Though hundreds of thousands of people may sign up to campaigns such as class action suits against tobacco companies, these are nonetheless individualistic endeavours albeit presented with a façade of group solidarity. Such individualized collective struggles attack injustices in a piecemeal, fractured manner, one corporation at a time. Ironically, this kind of action cannot prevail against the monolith of globalized capitalism as outlined in the globalization thesis. Our individual rights are said to be the only struggle open to us because we are fighting this 'new' order of globalization, where we no longer belong to any cohesive groups.

Menelik was sceptical of the concept of globalization:

> In reality even if they talk about globalization, we were the first people they use[d] as globalization, they spread us all over the place as slaves, so come on, they can't tell us nothing, once you are wise to the trickery of the society and its game.

Globalization is nothing new. The world cannot be much smaller than when Europeans wiped out the natives of the Caribbean then turned to Africa for the labour to provide them with unparalleled wealth. What is the Dutch East India Company, who enslaved countless Africans and used the massive profits to found the city of New York, if not a multinational company? The importance of the nation state during colonial times has also been overstated. For example, far from being in direct conflict with France during enslavement, Britain actually sustained the sugar production of her great rival by supplying French colonies with the enslaved (James, 1938). French enslavement could not have happened without this support. Globalization is an extension of the same Western imperialist project (Sivanandan, 2005). This is not to say that nothing has changed about the nature of capitalist society, but the fundamentally important relationship remains: the exploitation of the many by the few. The only way to seriously challenge injustice and inequality is for real, solid collectives to unite. As Kwame remarked about people in today's society, 'everybody wants to do it on their own, but you can't'.

The localized, grassroots Black supplementary school movement may seem an odd vehicle for a discussion of globalization. However, the construction of Blackness that is both globally defined and enacted on a local level is precisely the kind of collective identity required for contemporary activism. As explored in Chapters 3, 4, and 5, this commitment to Blackness does not limit the political responses and there has been major debate within the movement.

Official vs. self-help

Stone's (1981) distinction between official and self-help projects has been used to delineate the major fault line in the Black supplementary school movement, although there are projects that could be considered to sit on both sides of the divide. However, it does identify the main issue for the future of the movement. The trend has been for supplementary schools to become increasingly accommodated into mainstream school provision, obtaining their funds from educational authorities and focusing on the children's attainment in state schools. As the Extended Schools programme develops and mainstream schools continue to offer classes in the evenings and on Saturdays, models of supplementary schooling based solely on teaching mainstream subjects may become obsolete. Of course, the opposite may prove to be true. Conservative school policy, which looks set to fragment the school system, may well lead to a reversal of the progress in attainment made by Black children. If this happens, the need to reinforce the teaching of mainstream subjects in Black supplementary schools will again become a motivating factor for parents.

The nature of the radical sentiments expressed by certain of the self-help projects also needs to be considered. The radical approach that challenged the basis and authority of mainstream schooling has not entirely disappeared but is more commonly expressed today as the desire to design a cultural learning that is appropriate for Black students. The idea of African-centred education does represent a challenge to the values of mainstream schooling, but the goals remain the same: to produce students who are successful in society. African-centred education has spiritual elements that aim to build communal understandings and a world view that is a corrective to the ills of Western society. However, this element is not an alternative politics in itself and therefore does not offer a radical challenge. African-centred education can and may become accommodated into the mainstream school system. For the majority involved in both the African-centred and Black supplementary school movement, this may not be problematic, but it does place limitations on the criticality of the position.

Though the official and self-help traditions may seem to be somewhat competing and opposed, they in fact form different sides of a cohesive movement. Both involve communities coming together as Black people to safeguard the education of the young and to help them achieve mainstream school success. Of course, there are differences in the approach and philosophies behind how to do this, but, as Clive explained in his interview, 'it's the community isn't it, so you get a range of responses'.

Resisting racism

Given the history and tradition of Black supplementary schools in the community, it is certainly possible to deliver a Black education that both critiques and subverts, while at the same time helping students to navigate the mainstream school system. What is beyond doubt is that such an endeavour is essential. Though 'achievement' at school may be improving among Black students, there remains an entrenched disparity of outcomes, which indicates the racial disadvantage endemic in the system. The nature of the racism may change but the necessity remains for Black communities to create spaces for educating our children that are comfortable and free from the negative assumptions held by mainstream teachers. As a community we cannot expect, and certainly cannot depend on, the system to correct biases that have been in existence since Black children entered the British school system in large numbers decades ago. It is vital that we both maintain and create educational alternatives that can support Black children and call the mainstream to account through their successes.

Appendix

Interview schedule

ORGANIZATION
- Why was the project started?
- Aims and objectives of the school?
- When was it started? And how?
- How many pupils attend and how are they recruited?
- Age ranges of the students?
- How many teachers are there and how are they recruited?

CURRICULUM
- What subjects are taught at the school?
- Is there a focus on Black studies, culture, and history?
- How are the subjects taught decided?
- Are there any differences between the way classes are taught at the school and how they are taught in day-schools?

FUNDING
- How is the project funded?
- Is there support from LEA or state agencies? If so, what is your relationship with the LEA like?
- How do you feel about accepting money from state agencies? Does it compromise what you do?

PHILOSOPHY
- Why do parents bring their kids to the school? What are the benefits of school?
- Is there a problem with full-time schools?
- Can full-time schools successfully teach Black students?
- Is the school system still racist? Do Black students and families feel excluded?
- Do you see the role of the supplementary school as supporting mainstream education or acting as a replacement for what it cannot deliver?

BLACKNESS
- How important is having a predominantly Black school? How does it help learning?
- What does being Black mean? Why is Blackness important?

- Why is studying Black history and culture important?
- BLACK PRIDE
- Are there particular issues which Black students face that need to be addressed?
- What is the biggest problem facing Black people?
- Does the Black community play an important role in supporting the supplementary school?

Role of the church (if applicable)
- How important is the church to the supplementary school?
- Are religious studies part of the syllabus being taught?
- Could the supplementary school run without the church?

Future
- Have you had any difficulties with organizing the school? What are some of the challenges you have faced?
- What is the future for Black supplementary schools? For your school in particular?
- Do you have links to other supplementary schools? Is an umbrella organization required?
- Will Black supplementary schools play a significant role in the Black community in 15 years' time? How successful can they be when they serve relatively few students?
- What do you most need to support your supplementary school?
- Do we need separate Black full-time schools to adequately educate our young?

Debrief
- Is there anything you would like to add?
- Are there any questions that you think I should have asked, but didn't?
- Do you have any questions for me about what we have just discussed or the study itself?
- Remember you are free to withdraw from the study at any time, so if you change your mind about participating then just let me know.

Appendix

Table 1: Percentage of students receiving 5 A*–C grades (incl. maths and English) at GCSE level in 2010, by selected ethnicity, gender, and free school meals (DfE, 2007)

Ethnicity	Boys	Girls	Free school meals (both genders)	No free school meals (both genders)	Total
White	51.3	58.4	25.3	58.6	54.8
Black Caribbean	37	49.8	33.1	46.5	43.5
Black African	46.4	58.8	42.1	58.8	52.8
Black Other	40.5	51.4	34.9	50.1	45.8
White and Black Caribbean	41.5	48.9	30	50	45.3
White and Black African	53	58.4	37.8	60.4	55.6
Pakistani	45.3	53.1	40.6	53	49.1
Bangladeshi	45.3	58.1	50.3	56.6	53.7
Indian	67.7	75.2	55	73.2	71.3
Chinese	69.6	80.5	68.4	75.8	75.1
Average	51.1	58.6	30.9	58.5	54.8

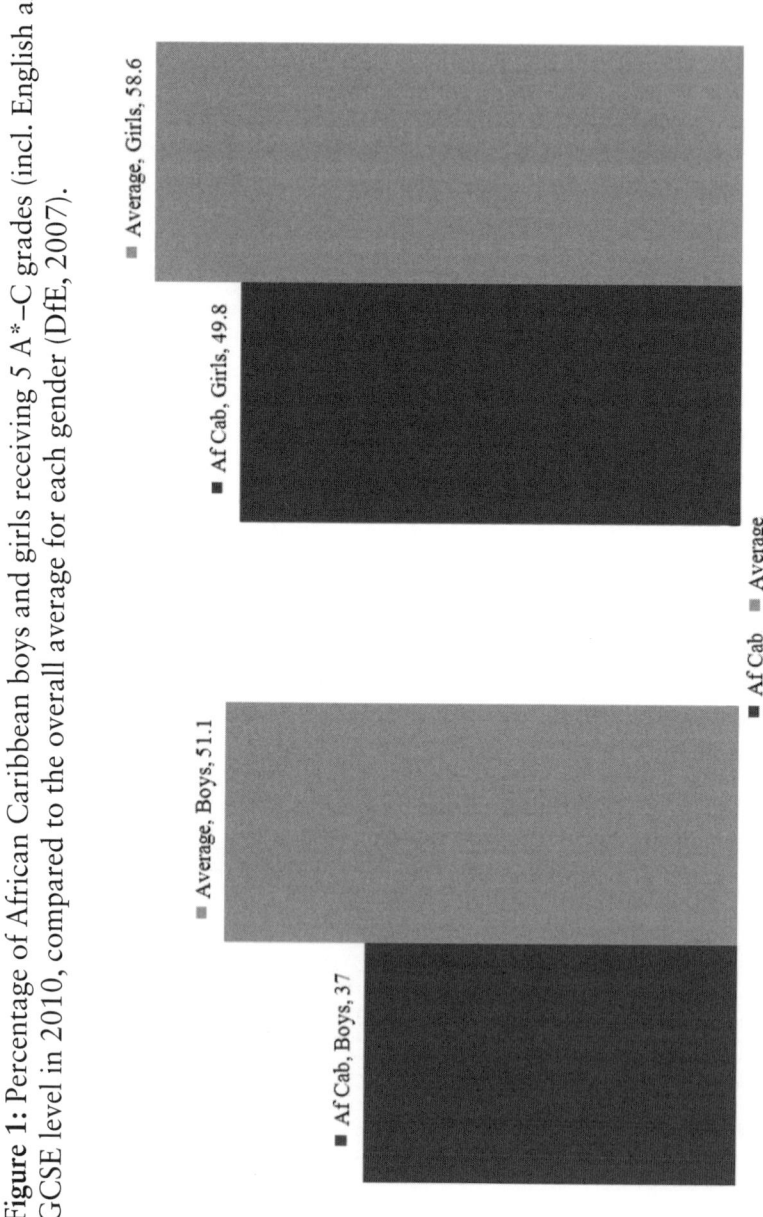

Figure 1: Percentage of African Caribbean boys and girls receiving 5 A*–C grades (incl. English and maths) at GCSE level in 2010, compared to the overall average for each gender (DfE, 2007).

References

Adams, L. and Kirova, A. (eds) (2006) *Global Migration and Education: School, children, and families*. New Jersey: Lawrence Erlbaum Associates.

Afridi, A. and Warmington, J. (2009) *The Pied Piper: The BME third sector and UK race relations policy*. Birmingham: Birmingham Race Action Partnership.

Alexander, C. (2002) 'Beyond black: Re-thinking the colour/culture divide'. *Ethnic and Racial Studies* 25(4) 552–71.

Alexander, C. and Alleyne, B. (2002) 'Introduction: Framing difference: racial and ethnic studies in twenty-first-century Britain'. *Ethnic and Racial Studies* 25(4) 541–51.

Alleyne, B. (2002) *Radicals Against Race*. Oxford: Berg.

Anderson, G.L. (1989) 'Critical ethnography in education: Origins, current status, and new directions'. *Review of Education Research* 59 249–70.

Asante, M.K. (2003) *Afrocentricity: The theory of social change*. Chicago: African American Images.

Association of Supplementary Schools (nd) Preamble. BPM 4/2/2/1(1). London: GPI Archive.

— (1987) 'Report on Supplementary Schools Conference, 8th April'. BPM 4/2/1/3(1). London: GPI Archive.

Atkinson, P. and Coffey, A. (2004) 'Analysing documentary realities'. In Silverman, D. (ed.) *Qualitative Research: Theory, method and practice*. London: Sage.

Back, L. (2007) *The Art of Listening*. Oxford: Berg.

Back, L., Keith, M., Khan, A., Shukra, K., and Solomos, J. (2002) 'The return of assimilationism: Race, multiculturalism and New Labour'. *Sociological Research Online* 7(2). www.socresonline.org.uk/7/2/back.html (August 2012).

Becker, H. (1967) 'Whose side are we on?' *Social Problems* 14 239–47.

Bell, D. (1992) *Faces at the Bottom of the Well: The permanence of racism*. New York: Basic Books.

Berthoud, R. (2000) 'Ethnic employment penalties in Britain'. *Journal of Ethic and Migration Studies* 26(3) 389–416.

Best, W. (1990) 'The Black supplementary school movement'. In Olowe, S. (ed.) *Against the Tide: Black experience in the ILEA*. London: Inner London Education Authority.

Biko, S. (1978) *I Write What I Like*. Johannesburg: Picador Africa. Repr., 2004.

Black Parents Movement (BPM) (nd) 'What is the Black Parents Movement?' BPM 1/1/1(1). London: GPI Archive.

— (1978) 'The history of the principles of organisation document and the policy committee – its work and decisions'. BPM 1/4/1/3(1). London: GPI Archive.

— (1981) 'Report to the training party, 26th October'. BPM 4/2/1/1(2). London: GPI Archive.

Black Students Movement (1978) 'Black Students Movement report'. BPM 1/1/2(1). London: GPI Archive.

Burawoy, M. (2005) '2004 American Sociological Association presidential address: For a public sociology'. *British Journal of Sociology* 56(2) 259–94.

Byfield, C. (2008) *Black Boys Can Make It: How they overcome the obstacles to university in the UK and USA*. Stoke on Trent: Trentham Books.

Cantle, T. (2001) *Community Cohesion: A report of the independent review team*. London: Home Office.

Carby, H. (1983) 'Schooling in Babylon'. In Centre for Contemporary Cultural Studies (ed.) *The Empire Strikes Back*. London: Hutchinson.

Caribbean Education and Community Workers Association (nd) 'Caribbean Education and Community Workers Association constitution'. BEM 2/2/1/2(1). London: GPI Archive.

— (1971) 'Newsletter'. BEM 3/1/4/1(42). London: GPI Archive.

Caribbean Educationists Association (1970) 'Report on the formation of the Caribbean Educationists Association'. BEM 2/2/1/1(2). London: GPI Archive.

Carmichael, S. (1971) *Stokely Speaks: Black Power to Pan-Africanism*. New York: Vintage Books.

Carmichael, S. and Hamilton, C.V. (1969) *Black Power: The politics of liberation in America*. Harmondsworth: Penguin.

Carter, P. (2003) 'Black cultural capital, status positioning and schooling conflicts for low income African American youth'. *Social Problems* 50(1) 136–55.

Chevannes, M. and Reeves, F. (1989) 'The black voluntary school movement: Definition, context and prospects'. In Troyna, B. (ed.) *Racial Inequality in Education*. London: Routledge.

Clark, K.B. and Clark, M.P. (1940) 'Skin colour as a factor in racial identification and preferences in Negro children'. *Journal of Experimental Education* 8 161–3.

Coard, B. (1971) *How the West Indian Child is Made Educationally Subnormal in the British School System*. London: New Beacon Books.

Cole, M. (2003) 'Ethnicity, "status groups" and racialization: A contribution to a debate on national identity in Britain'. *Ethnic and Racial Studies* 26(5) 962–9.

— (2004) '"Brutal and stinking" and "difficult to handle": The historical and contemporary manifestations of racialisation, institutional racism, and schooling in Britain'. *Race Ethnicity and Education* 7(1) 35–56.

Comprehension (nd) 'Comprehension in Pan African History'. BEM 3/1/5/11. London: GPI Archive.

ContinYou (2011) 'The Quality Framework'. www.continyou.org.uk/what_we_do/supplementary_education/quality_framework/ (August 2012).

Creese, A., Bhatt, A., Bhojani, N., and Martin, P. (2008) 'Fieldnotes in team ethnography: Researching complementary schools'. *Qualitative Research* 8 197–215.

Crenshaw, K.W. (1995) 'Race, reform and retrenchment: Transformation and legitimation in anti-discrimination law'. In Crenshaw, K.W., Gotanda, N., Peller, G., and Thomas, K. (eds) *Critical Race Theory: The key writings that formed the movement*. New York: The New Press.

Cronon, E. (1969) *Black Moses: The story of Marcus Garvey*. Madison, WI: The University of Wisconsin Press.

Cross, W.E. (1971) 'The Negro to Black conversion experience'. *Black World* 20 13–27.

— (1991) *Shades of Black: Diversity in African American identity*. Philadelphia. PA: Temple University Press.

References

Daly, M. (2003) 'My life as a secret policeman'. *BBC News Magazine*. news.bbc.co.uk/1/hi/magazine/3210614.stm (August 2012).

D'Apolitio, R. (2000) 'The active role of the Black church: A theoretical analysis and empirical investigation of one contemporary active Black church'. *Journal of Black Studies* 31(1) 96–123.

Davis, A. (1982) *Women, Race and Class*. London: The Women's Press.

Department for Education (DfE) (2007) 'GCSE results by ethnicity'. www.education.gov.uk/rsgateway/DB/SFR/s000759/index.shtml (March 2012).

— (2011) 'New Free Schools are a popular choice for parents with latest analysis showing that half are in the 30 per cent most deprived communities'. www.education.gov.uk/inthenews/inthenews/a00197713/new-free-schools-are-a-popular-choice-for-parents-with-latest-analysis-showing-that-half-are-in-the-30-per-cent-most-deprived-communities (August 2012).

Doulton, A.J.F. (1969) 'Haringey comprehensive schools'. BEM 1/2/5(16). London: GPI Archive.

Dove, D. (1991) 'Investigative research: Is there a case for Black schooling?' BPM 4/2/4/1(1). London: GPI Archive.

Dove, N.E. (1993) 'The emergence of Black supplementary schools: Resistance to racism in the UK'. *Urban Education* 27(4) 430–47.

Dyson, M.E. (2000) *I May Not Get There with You: The true Martin Luther King, Jr.* New York: Touchstone.

— (2005) *Is Bill Cosby Right?: Or has the Black middle class lost its mind?* New York: Basic Civitas Books.

Ealing Community Relations Council (nd) 'The secondary school curriculum'. BEM 3/1/5/1(2). London: GPI Archive.

Evans, G. (1997) 'Political ideology and popular beliefs about class and inequality: Evidence from a survey experiment'. *The British Journal of Sociology* 48(3) 450–70.

Figueroa, P. (1991) *Education and the Social Construction of Race*. London: Routledge.

Freire, P. (1972) *The Pedagogy of the Oppressed*. Harmondsworth: Penguin Education.

— (1985) *The Politics of Education: Culture, power, and liberation*. Westport, C.T.: Bergin and Garvey Publishers.

Garvey, M. (1923) *The Philosophy and Opinions of Marcus Garvey: Or Africa for the Africans*. London: Routledge. Repr., 1967.

Gillborn, D. (2008) *Racism and Education: Coincidence or conspiracy*. Oxon: Routledge.

Gillen, P. and Ghosh, D. (2007) *Colonialism and Modernity*. Sydney: New South Wales Press.

Gilroy, P. (1998) 'Race ends here'. *Ethnic and Racial Studies* 21(5) 838–47.

— (2002) *The Black Atlantic: Modernity and double consciousness*. London: Verso.

Graham, M. (2001) 'The "miseducation" of Black children in the British educational system – towards an African-centred orientation to knowledge'. In Majors, R. (ed.) *Educating Our Black Children: New directions and approaches*. London: RoutledgeFalmer.

Gran, P. (1996) *Beyond Eurocentrism: A new view of modern world history*. Syracuse: Syracuse University Press.

Grosvenor, I. (1997) *Assimilating Identities: Racism and educational policy in post 1945 Britain*. London: Lawrence and Wishart.

Hall, K.A., Özerk, K., Zulfiqar, M., and Tan, J.E.C. (2002) 'This is our school: Provision, purpose and pedagogy of supplementary schooling in Leeds and Oslo'. *British Education Research Journal* 28(3) 399–418.

Hall, S. (1991) 'Old and new identities, old and new ethnicities'. In King, A.D. (ed.) *Culture, Globalization and the World-System: Contemporary conditions for the representation of identity*. Binghamton: New York Press.

— (1993) 'Culture, community, nation'. *Cultural Studies* 7(3) 349–63.

— (2007) 'The West and the rest: Discourse and power'. In Gupta, T.D. (ed.) *Race and Racialisation: Essential readings*. Toronto: Canadian Scholars Press.

Hammersley, M. (1985) 'From ethnography to theory: A programme and paradigm in the sociology of education'. *Sociology* 19 244–59.

Harris, A.L. (1927) 'Economic foundations of American race division'. *Social Forces* 5(3) 468–74.

Hart, R. (nd) 'A position paper for consideration of the Steering Committee of the West Indian Education and Welfare Association'. BEM 3/2/1/1(22). London: GPI Archive.

Henry, W. (2006) *What the Deejay Said: A critique from the street!* London: Nu Beyond Ltd.

— (2007) *Whiteness Made Simple*. London: Learning By Choice.

Hill Collins, P. (2000) *Black Feminist Thought: Knowledge, consciousness, and the politics of empowerment*. London: Routledge.

Hilliard, A. (1998) *SBA: The reawakening of the African mind*. Gainesville: Makare Publishing.

Hirsh, A. (2009) 'Watchdog split over Trevor Phillips leadership and remit'. *Guardian Unlimited*. www.guardian.co.uk/uk/2009/jul/20/trevor-phillips-watchdog-split-leadership?intcmp=239 (August 2012).

Home Office (1973) 'Urban Aid circular'. BEM 3/1/4/1(36). London: GPI Archive.

Homework (nd) 'Homework of a student at the George Padmore School'. BEM 3/1/6/1(16). London: GPI Archive.

Howarth, C. (2004) 'Re-presentation and resistance in the context of school exclusion: Reasons to be critical'. *Journal of Community and Applied Social Psychology* 14 356–77.

Hylton, C. (1999) *African-Caribbean Community Organisations: The search for individual and group identity*. Stoke on Trent: Trentham Books.

Illich, I. (1973) *Deschooling Society*. Harmondsworth: Penguin Education.

International Labour Office (1999) *Migrant Workers: Internal Labour Conference, 87th session*. Geneva: International Labour Office.

Issa, T. and Williams, C. (2009) *Realising Potential: Complementary schools in the UK*. Stoke on Trent: Trentham Books.

Jackson, A. (2006) *The British Empire and the Second World War*. London: Continuum.

Jackson, J.G. (1970) *Introduction to African Civilizations*. New York: University Books.

James, C.L.R (1938) *The Black Jacobins*. London: Penguin. Repr., 2001.

References

Jenkins, R. (2005) 'The place of theory: John Rex's contribution to the sociological study of "race"'. *Ethnic and Racial Studies* 28(2) 201–11.

John, G. (1987) 'A movement in search of a focus'. National Association of Multicultural Education. BPM 4/3/2/2(1). London: GPI Archive.

— (2005) 'This conflict has been 30 years in the making'. *Guardian Unlimited.* www.guardian.co.uk/uk/2005/oct/26/ukcrime.race (November 2012).

— (2006) *Taking a Stand: Gus John speaks on education, race, social action and civil unrest 1980–2005.* Manchester: Gus John Partnership.

Jones, V. (1987) 'Report on Supplementary Schools Conference, 8th April'. BPM 4/2/1/3(1). London: GPI Archive.

Judy, R.A.T. (1994) 'On the question of Nigga authenticity'. *boundary 2* 29(3) 211–30.

Kalra, V.S. and Kapoor, N. (2009) 'Interrogating segregation, integration and the community cohesion agenda'. *Journal of Ethnic and Migration Studies* 35(9) 1,397–415.

Kelley, R. and Esch, B. (1999) 'Black like Mao: Red China and black revolution'. *Souls* 1(4) 6–41.

Kilcup, K. (2000) *Native American Women's Writing 1800–1924: An anthology.* Oxford: Blackwell.

Killian, L.M. (1979) 'School busing in Britain: Policies and perceptions'. *Harvard Educational Review* 49(2) 185–206.

King, K.L., Houston, I.S., and Middleton, R.A. (2001) 'An explanation for Black school failure: Moving beyond Black inferiority and alienation as a policy agenda'. *British Journal of Educational Studies* 49(4) 428–45.

King, M.L. (1963) 'I Have a Dream'. *American Rhetoric.* www.americanrhetoric.com/speeches/mlkihaveadream.htm (August 2012).

— (1969) *Chaos or community?* Harmondsworth: Pelican Books.

Klem, A.M. and Connell, J.P. (2004) 'Relationships matter: Linking teacher support to student engagement and achievement'. *Journal of School Health* 74(7) 262–73.

Kundani, A. (2002) 'The death of multiculturalism'. *Race and Class* 43 67–72.

LaGroan, K.L. (2000) 'From minstrelsy to Gangsta Rap: The "Nigger" as a commodity for popular American entertainment'. *Journal of African American Studies* 5(2) 117–31.

La Rose, J. (1976) 'Letter to Community Development Unit, Haringey'. BEM 3/1/2/3(14). London: GPI Archive.

Leach, C.W. (2005) 'Against the notion of a "new racism"'. *Journal of Community and Applied Social Psychology* 15(6) 432–45.

Lemelle, S.J. (1993) 'The politics of cultural existence: Pan-Africanism, historical materialism and Afrocentricity'. *Race and Class* 35(1) 93–112.

Levy, A. (2004) *Small Island.* London: Headline Book Publishing.

Lincoln, Y.S. and Guba, E.G. (1985) *Naturalistic Inquiry.* Newbury Park, CA: Sage.

London Borough of Haringey (1969) 'Report from the London Borough of Haringey'. BEM 1/2/5(13). London: GPI Archive.

Lorde, A. (1984) *Sister Outsider.* Berkeley: The Crossing Press.

Macpherson, W. (1999) *The Stephen Lawrence Inquiry.* London: Her Majesty's Stationery Office.

Mahoney, K. and Noel, M. (2012) *The Descendants: Echoes from the past*. London: Grimoire Books.

Mandela, N.R. (1996) *Long Walk to Freedom*. London: Abacus Books.

Martin, B.L. (1991) 'From Negro to Black to African American: The power of names and naming'. *Political Science Quarterly* 106(1) 83–107.

Martin, P., Crease, A., and Bhatt, A. (2003) 'Complementary schools and their communities in Leicester'. *Final Report for the ESRC for Project No: R000223949*.

Martinez, T.A. (1997) 'Popular culture as oppositional culture: Rap as resistance'. *Sociological Perspectives* 40(2) 265–86.

Mason, D. (1995) *Race and Ethnicity in Modern Britain*. Oxford: Oxford University Press.

McGhee, D. (2005) *Intolerant Britain?: Hate, citizenship and difference*. Maidenhead: Open University Press.

Methodist Church, Clapham (1982) 'Black supplementary school'. BPM 4/2/3/2. London: GPI Archive.

Miles, R. and Brown, M. (2003) *Racism*. London: Routledge.

Milner, H.R. (2007) 'Race, culture, and research positionality: Working through dangers seen, unseen, and unforseen'. *Educational Researcher* 36 388–400.

— (2008) 'Critical Race Theory and interest convergence as analytic tools in teacher education policies and practices'. *Journal of Teacher Education* 59 332–46.

Mirza, H.S. and Reay, D. (2000) 'Spaces and places of Black educational desire: Rethinking Black supplementary schools as a new social movement'. *Sociology* 34(3) 521–44.

Modood, T. (1994) 'Political blackness and British Asians'. *Sociology* 28(4) 859–76.

— (1996) 'If races do not exist'. In Barot, R. (ed.) *The Racism Problematic: Contemporary sociological debates on race and ethnicity*. Lewiston/Queenston/Lampeter: The Edward Mellen Press.

— (2005) *Multicultural Politics: Racism, ethnicity and Muslims in Britain*. Bodmin: MPG Books.

Muir, H. (20 August 2007) 'Black army officers recruited to stop gang violence'. *Guardian*. www.guardian.co.uk/uk/2007/aug/20/ukcrime.race.

Munck, R. (2002) *Globalisation and Labour: The great new transformation?* London: Zed Books.

Murray, C.H. (1990) *The Emerging British Underclass*. London: Institute of Economic Affairs.

Mutwa, V.C. (1998) *Indaba My Children: African tribal history*. Edinburgh: Payback Press.

National Association of Black Supplementary Schools (1982) 'Letter, 20th January'. BPM 4/2/1/2(1). London: GPI Archive.

— (1987) 'Report on Supplementary Schools Conference, 8th April'. BPM 4/2/1/3(1). London: GPI Archive.

— (2011) 'History/aims and objectives'. www.nabss.org.uk/#/historyaims-objectives/4551182236 (April 2012).

Nayak, A. (2006) 'After race: Ethnography, race and post-race theory'. *Ethnic and Racial Studies* 29(3) 411–30.

References

Nazroo, J.Y. and Karlsen, S. (2003) 'Patterns of identity among ethnic minority people: Diversity and commonality'. *Ethnic and Racial Studies* 26(5) 902–30.

Nettleford, R.M. (1970) *Mirror, Mirror: Identity, race and protest in Jamaica*. Kingston: LMH Publishing. Repr., 1998.

Niro, B. (2003) *Race*. Basingstoke: Palgrave Macmillan.

Nkrumah, K. (1963) *Africa Must Unite*. London: Panaf Books. Repr., 1998.

Noblit, G.W. (1984) 'The prospects of an applied ethnography for education: A sociology of knowledge interpretation'. *Educational Evaluation and Policy Analysis* 6(1) 95–101.

North London West Indian Association (nd) Leaflet. BEM 1/2/5(100). London: GPI Archive.

— (1969a) 'Certain proposals of the NLWIA concerning education in Haringey'. BEM 1/2/5(26). London: GPI Archive.

— (1969b) 'NLWIA leaflet rejecting banding proposals'. BEM1/2/5(8). London: GPI Archive.

— (1969c) 'Petition against banding'. BEM 1/2/5(28). London: GPI Archive.

Office for National Statistics (2004) 'Social Trends: no. 34'. Norwich: Her Majesty's Stationery Office.

— (2011) 'Population estimates by ethnic group 2002–2009'. www.ons.gov.uk/ons/taxonomy/index.html?nscl=Population+Estimates+by+Ethnic+Group (August 2012).

Ogbu, J.U. (2004) 'Collective identity and the burden of "acting White" in Black history, community and education'. *Urban Review* 36(1) 1–35.

Panorama (2008) 'When David Cameron met the undecided'. BBC. news.bbc.co.uk/1/hi/programmes/panorama/7642749.stm, accessed 23 August 2012.

Parekh, B. (2000) *The Future of Multi-ethnic Britain: The Parekh Report*. London: Profile Books.

Parsons, C. (2009) 'Explaining sustained inequalities in ethnic minority school exclusion in England – passive racism in a neoliberal grip'. *Race, Ethnicity and Education* 35(2) 249–65.

Pearson, D.G. (1978) 'Race, religiosity and political activism: Some observations of West Indian Participation in Britain'. *The British Journal of Sociology* 29(3) 340–57.

Peller, G. (1995) 'Race-consciousness'. In Crenshaw, K.W., Gotanda, N., Peller, G., and Thomas, K. (eds) *Critical Race Theory: The key writings that formed the movement*. New York: The New Press.

Peter Moses Supplementary School (nd) Report. BPM 4/2/3/1. London: GPI Archive.

Phillips, M. and Phillips, T. (1998) *Windrush: The irresistible rise of multi-racial Britain*. London: HarperCollins.

Pollard, D.S. and Ajirotutu, C.S. (2001) 'Lessons from America: The African American immersion schools experience'. In Majors, R. (ed.) *Educating Our Black Children: New directions and approaches*. London: RoutledgeFalmer.

Preissle, J. and Grant, L. (1998) 'Exploring the ethnography of education'. *Journal of Contemporary Ethnography* 27(3) 3–9.

Quinn, E. (2000) 'Black British cultural studies and the rap on Gangsta'. *Black Music Research Journal* 20(2) 195–216.

Ramesh, R. (2012) 'Black people more likely to be jobless in Britain than US, research reveals'. *Guardian Unlimited*. www.guardian.co.uk/world/2012/apr/13/black-people-unemployed-britain-us (April 2012).

Rampton, A. (1981) *West Indian Children in Our Schools*. London: Her Majesty's Stationery Office.

Reay, D. and Mirza, H.S. (1997) 'Uncovering genealogies of the margins: Black supplementary schooling'. *British Journal of Sociology of Education* 18(4) 477–99.

Reeves, F. and Chevannes, M. (1983a) 'The ideological construction of Black underachievement'. *Multi-Racial Education* 12(1) 22–41.

— (1983b) *Notes on the Development of a Black Supplementary School*. Wolverhampton: Afro-Caribbean Education Trust.

Reynolds, T. (2001) 'Black mothering, paid work and identity'. *Ethnic and Racial Studies* 24(6) 1,046–64.

Robinson, C.J. (1983) *Black Marxism: The making of the Black radical tradition*. London: Zed Books.

Rock, C. (2002) *Bring the Pain*. DVD, Glendale, CA: Dreamworks Productions.

Roy, A. (2003) *War Talk*. Cambridge, MA: South End Press.

Said, E. (2003) *Orientalism*. London: Penguin Books.

Scobie, E. (1972) *Black Britannia: A history of Blacks in Britain*. Chicago, IL: Johnson Publishing Company.

Seale, B. (1970) *Seize the Time: The story of the Black Panther Party*. New York: Random House.

Sealy, C. (1974) 'The reorganisation of supplementary schools'. 18th April. BEM 3/2/1/1(2). London: GPI Archive.

Sellers, R.M., Smith, M.A., Shelton, J.N., Rowley, A.J., and Chavous, T.M. (1998) 'Multidimensional Model of Racial Identity: A reconceptualisation of African American racial identity'. *Personality and Social Psychology Review* 2(1) 18–39.

Sewell, T. (2009) *Generating Genius: Black boys in search of love, ritual and schooling*. Stoke on Trent: Trentham Books.

Shukra, K. (1998) *The Changing Pattern of Black Politics in Britain*. London: Pluto Press.

Sivanandan, A. (2005) 'Race and class: The future'. *Race & Class* 46(3) 1–6.

Smith, J.A., Flowers, P., and Larkin, M. (2009) *Interpretative Phenomenological Analysis: Theory, method and research*. London: Sage.

Sprance, W.R. (2008) 'The new tournament of shadows: The strategic implications of China's activity in Sub-Saharan Africa and Africom's role in the U.S. response'. *Journal of Military and Strategic Studies* 10(3) 1–19.

Steven, P.A.J. (2007) 'Researching race/ethnicity and educational inequality in English secondary schools: A critical review of the research literature between 1980 and 2005'. *Review of Educational Research* 77(2) 147–85.

St Louis, B. (2002) 'Post-race/post-politics?: Activist-intellectualism and the reification of race'. *Ethnic and Racial Studies* 25(4) 652–75.

Stone, M. (1981) *The Education of the Black Child in Britain*. London: Fontana.

Sudbury, J. (2001) '(Re)constructing multi-racial blackness: Women's activism, difference and collective identity in Britain'. *Ethnic and Racial Studies* 24(1) 29–49.

References

Sundiata Liberation Center for Children (1969) 'Position paper, October'. BEM 3/2/1/1(15). London: GPI Archive.

Supplementary Schools Conference (1987) 'Report on Supplementary Schools Conference: Funded and hosted by ILEA'. BPM 4/2/1/3(1). London: GPI Archive.

Swann, M. (1985) *Education for All*. London: Her Majesty's Stationery Office.

Tiejun, W. (2007) 'Deconstructing modernization'. *Chinese Sociology and Anthropology* 39(4) 10–25.

Tomlinson, S. (1988) 'The "Black Education" movement'. In Arnot, M. (ed.) *Race and Gender: Equal opportunities in education*. Oxford: Pergamon Press.

Troyna, B. and Williams, J. (1986) *Racism, Education and the State*. London: Biddles.

Tucker, J. (2004) *A Sense of Wonder: Samuel R. Delany, race, identity and difference*. Middletown: Wesleyan University Press.

Tutu, D. (2000) *No Future Without Forgiveness*. New York: Doubleday.

Upchurch, C. (1997) *Convicted in the Womb: One man's journey from prisoner to peacemaker*. New York: Bantam Books.

Vertovec, S. (2002) 'Islamaphobia and Muslim recognition in Britain'. In Hadda, Y.Y. (ed.) *Muslims in the West: From sojourners to citizens*. New York: Oxford University Press.

Walvin, J. (2001) *Black Ivory: Slavery in the British Empire*. Oxford: Blackwell Publishers.

Warren, N. (1990) 'Pan-African cultural movements: From Baraka to Karenga'. *The Journal of Negro History* 75(1/2) 16–28.

Warsama, M. (2007) *Roots Remembered*. DVD, London: BBC.

West, C. (1993) *Keeping Faith: Philosophy and race in America*. London: Routledge.

West Indian Educationists (nd) 'Final session of the West Indian Educationists'. BEM 2/2/1/1(24). London: GPI Archive.

West Indian Standing Conference (1970) 'West Indian Standing Conference: The last three years'. BEM 2/1/4. London: GPI Archive.

Williams, E. (1975) *Capitalism and Slavery*. London: Andre Deutsch.

Willis, P. (1977) *Learning to Labour: How working class kids get working class jobs*. Farnborough: Saxon House.

Wilson, A. (1978) *The Developmental Psychology of the Black Child*. New York: Africana Research Publications.

— (1994) *Black on Black Violence: The psychodynamics of Black self-annihilation in the service of white domination*. New York: Afrikan World Infosystems.

Wiltshire, B. (1987) 'Report on Supplementary Schools Conference, 8th April'. BPM 4/2/1/3(1). London: GPI Archive.

Worley, C. (2005) '"It's not about race. It's about the community": New Labour and "community cohesion"'. *Critical Social Policy* 25(4) 483–96.

Wright, R. (2008) *Black Power: Three books from exile: Black Power; The Color Curtain; And White Man, Listen!* New York: HarperCollins.

X, M. (1965) *The Autobiography of Malcolm X*. London: Penguin Books.

— (1970) *By Any Means Necessary*. New York: Pathfinder Press.

— (1971) *The End of White World Supremacy: Four speeches*. New York: Merlin House.

Yekwai, D. (1998) *British Racism, Miseducation and the Afrikan Child*. London: Karnak House.

Young, V.A. (2004) 'Your average Nigga'. *College Composition and Communication* 55(4) 693–715.

Younge, G. (1999) *No Place Like Home: A Black Briton's journey through the American South*. London: Picador.

Zack-Williams, A.B. (1997) 'African Diaspora conditioning: The case of Liverpool'. *Journal of Black Studies* 27(4) 528–42.

Index

accommodative resistance, 62, 75, 89
accreditation, 20, 47–8, 60, 81
African British population, 29–31
African centred education, 34, 75, 81–3, 85–9, 135
African National Congress (ANC), 31
Association of Supplementary Schools, 45, 53
attainment in mainstream schools, 29–30, 46–50, 56, 84, 135

Bandung Conference, 34
Biko, Steve, 31
Black history, 5–6, 16, 29, 48–9, 51, 54–6, 72, 80–1, 84, 100, 104, 105, 108–118, 123, 125–8, 130, 133, 137
Black identity, 3, 6, 25–7, 30, 36–8, 115, 135
Black independent schools, 20, 75, 83–8, 93
Black Panthers, 19, 45, 83, 88,
Black Parents Movement, 13, 15, 32, 52–3, 58
Black Power, 25, 27, 45
Black pride, 61, 71–2, 77, 80, 84, 100, 102–4, 108, 100, 112, 114–5, 126–7, 138
Black Youth/Student Movement, 13
Black-led churches, 18, 21, 60–3, 138
Black environment, 55–9, 85, 88, 102, 115, 120, 125
Bogle, Paul, 125

Caribbean Education and Community Workers Association, 4, 10, 13–4, 18, 28, 49
Carmichael, Stokely, 26, 33
Civil Rights movement, 27, 54, 61–2
Coard, Bernard, 4–6, 10, 19
colonialism, 1, 23–4, 34, 71, 106
colour blindness, 23, 59
community cohesion, 55–6, 86
ContinYou, 20, 47–8, 81
Cross, William, 26, 36
cultural capital, 5, 78

Diaspora, 28, 32, 34–6, 82, 96, 115, 117, 133

educationally subnormal, 4–5, 11, 63
enslavement, 22–5, 29, 60, 80, 83, 102, 106–10, 112,–3, 115, 125–7, 134
ethnography, 93, 95–8
eurocentrism, 24, 75, 79, 81, 83, 85, 102,

free schools, 87
Freire, Paolo, 52, 79, 94, 121,

Garvey, Marcus, 19, 25–6, 102, 104–5, 108
George Padmore and Albertina Sylvester Schools, 16–19, 44, 49, 50
George Padmore Institute, 7, 10–13, 18
globalization, 133–5

Hall, Stuart, 27, 32, 37
hidden curriculum, 80

Illich, Ivan, 78
individualism, 68, 71, 73–4, 87, 132
Inner London Education Authority, 16, 44–5, 53, 58
institutional racism, 64, 69–71, 97
IQ tests, 5–6, 11–12

Jackson, George, 19, 50
John, Gus, 14

Kwanzaa, 102–3

La Rose, John, 10, 16

Marxism, 22–3, 35, 96, 124
migration, 1, 4, 7, 26–7, 30, 126
multiculturalism, 55–6, 80

Nanny of the Maroons, 109–10, 112
National Association of Black Supplementary Schools, viii, 19, 20, 41, 53, 129
National Association of Multicultural Education, 14
negritude, 112
New Beacon bookshop, 10–13, 16, 18, 52–3, 132
Nigger/Nigga, 25, 75–6
non-Whiteism, 33
North London West Indian Association, 4, 11–13

oppositional culture, 77–8

Pan-Africanism, 52, 92, 99, 102, 115
political blackness, 31–5

Queen Nzinga, 105–6, 128

racialization, 22
role of parents, 61, 68–9, 87, 104, 107–8, 110–11, 115, 130–3
role models, 65–7, 130

Seacole, Mary, 111–13
self-esteem, 6–7, 49, 66, 72, 73–4, 77, 81, 106
state funding, 17–8, 39, 43–7, 49, 54–56, 60, 63, 93, 118–9, 137

teacher-student relationship, 46, 61–2, 101, 103, 116, 118, 120–1, 131

underachievement, 7, 60, 63–69, 74, 130

West Indian Educationists, 51
West Indian Standing Conference, 13, 28, 31
West Indian Welfare and Education Association, 71,
Whiteness, 33–4
Wilson, Amos, 66, 72

X, Malcolm, 25–6, 61–2, 103, 113–5